SKILL SHARPENERS
Geography
6

Writing: Mike Graf
Editing: Lisa Vitarisi Mathews
Copy Editing: Cathy Harber
Art Direction: Yuki Meyer
Design/Production: Yuki Meyer
Jessica Onken

EMC 3746

Evan-Moor.
Helping Children Learn

Visit
teaching-standards.com
to view a correlation
of this book.
This is a free service.

**Correlated to
Current Standards**

Contents

Essential Element: The World in Spatial Terms

Unit 1 5
- Pinpoint Radar
- Winds on Earth
- Hurricanes and Typhoons
- Storms on Earth
- Weather Report
- More Than Just Weather

Unit 2 13
- City Lights at Night
- One Square Inch
- Aurora Borealis
- Special Places on Earth
- Your Own Quiet Spot
- Star Gazing

Unit 3 21
- Mexico City
- Three Cities in Asia
- Not a Soul in Sight
- Lots of People or Not?
- I Want to Visit . . .
- Large City or Small Town?

Essential Element: Places and Regions

Unit 4 29
- We Won the Lottery!
- A Trip to Iceland
- High-Elevation Capital
- How Much Sun?
- Graphing Sunlight
- A Letter Home

Unit 5 37
- Can You Keep a Secret?
- Three Great Trees
- Upside-Down Tree
- Where Are the Trees?
- Adopt a Tree
- The Most Unusual Trees

Unit 6 45
- Ancient Gondwanaland
- A United Germany
- Sharing a Continent
- Managing Lands
- Sign a Treaty
- Changing Spaces

Essential Element: Physical Systems

Unit 7 53

- Reporting from the Galápagos
- Colliding Plates
- Landforms on Earth
- Places on Earth
- Landform Maps
- New Landforms

Unit 8 61

- Life in Death Valley
- Las Vegas, The Meadows
- Oasis in the Desert
- Water Is Essential
- Oasis Diorama
- A Very Rare Place

Essential Element: Human Systems

Unit 9 69

- High-Altitude Superhumans
- Breathing at the Top of the World
- Desert Wanderers
- Nomadic People
- A Day in the Life
- Choose Your Life

Unit 10 77

- My Irish Roots
- Angel Island
- Shelter in Europe
- Immigration
- Family History Maps
- A Long Journey

Unit 11 85

- Holiday Panic
- The Euro
- A Barrel of Oil
- World Currency
- Exchanging Money
- Other Currencies

Unit 12 93

- I Am Roald Amundsen
- A Special Lake
- Who Owns the Oceans?
- By Land or By Sea?
- UNESCO World Heritage Sites
- A Protected Place Near You

Contents, continued

Essential Element: Environment and Society

Unit 13 101
- My First Scuba Dive
- A City Built on Water
- More Water Needed!
- Dealing with Water
- What's Changed?
- Water Works

Unit 14 109
- Goodbye, Cars!
- Fracking
- Oh Canada!
- Changing Resources
- City Planning
- Can Car-Free Work for Everyone?

Essential Element: The Uses of Geography

Unit 15 117
- The Warship *Vasa*
- Sea Pirates
- Sunken Treasures
- Sea Travel
- Craft Stick Boat
- Ship Safety

Unit 16 125
- Weird Things Found in Ice
- Goodbye, Ice
- Where Is the Ice?
- It's All About the Ice
- A Chunk of Glacial Ice
- Signs of Warmth

Answer Key 133

Pinpoint Radar

Concept:
Maps are created to provide specific information.

I have been interested in weather for as long as I can remember. Now I help the weathercaster at my local television station in Kansas. I make some of the graphics he uses in the weather report.

Last week, my job at the station took an unexpected turn. I was there as usual on Friday afternoon, when the station sent the main weathercaster out into the field to broadcast live. Severe weather was coming in. That meant I would have to make some of the weather graphics, as well as switch them from one to the next during the broadcast.

I made a radar loop of the tornado coming toward our town. The meteorologist gave the report and I flipped the graphics one by one. First, it was a sweeping view of our city with the band of thunderstorms. The red and orange colors indicated the heavier precipitation coming toward us. The radar loop showed where the tornado was. The loop of the last hour clearly showed that the storm was coming from the southwest and moving toward the northeast. Then when we got to the latest radar graphic, I was able to zoom in. It showed a pinpoint mapped location of where the storm was now. We could also project where it was going. I zoomed the radar all the way down to street level. I could see neighborhoods, and mine was one of them! I knew this broadcast was helping people to prepare for the tornado.

The World in Spatial Terms

Winds on Earth

Concept:
Maps are created to provide specific information.

The World in Spatial Terms

Define It!

jet stream: winds in Earth's upper atmosphere

atmosphere: the air surrounding Earth

trade winds: the cycle of wind currents moving away from the equator and back

Most tornadoes in the United States move from the southwest to the northeast. One of the reasons for this is that they are driven by the jet stream, or the upper atmosphere wind pattern. Movement of air within Earth's atmosphere is called wind. The main cause of wind is the sun heating the ground unevenly. When this happens, it changes the air pressure, which produces areas of high pressure and low pressure. Wind blows from areas of high pressure to low pressure, which can help produce and drive storms. Wind is also determined by mountains, lakes, canyons, beaches, and other factors.

The sun heats the area around the equator more than at the poles. Warm air at the equator rises and moves toward the poles. As the rising air moves away from the equator, it cools and drops back down to Earth. This cycle is called the trade winds.

The jet stream winds in the upper atmosphere can blow at speeds of about 100 miles per hour (161 kph). The jet stream moves mostly from west to east due to Earth's rotation. But it can fluctuate, or move around. Weather forecasters use the jet stream to determine storm movement. Pilots also use the jet stream—flying with the jet stream can reduce air travel time, but flying against it can take longer.

Answer the items.

1. How does heat cause wind?

_____

_____

2. What other professions might use the jet stream to help them?

_____

_____

Skill Sharpeners: Geography • EMC 3746 • © Evan-Moor Corp.

Wind Patterns

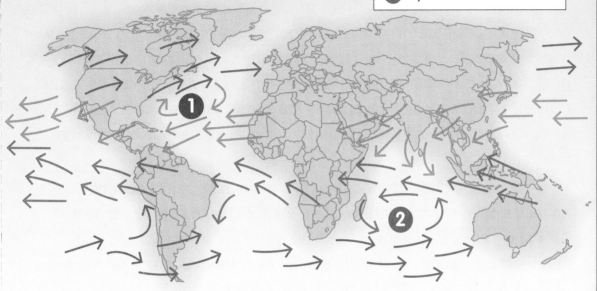

← westerlies
← trade winds (northeasterly)
← trade winds (southeasterly)
1 hurricanes
2 cyclones

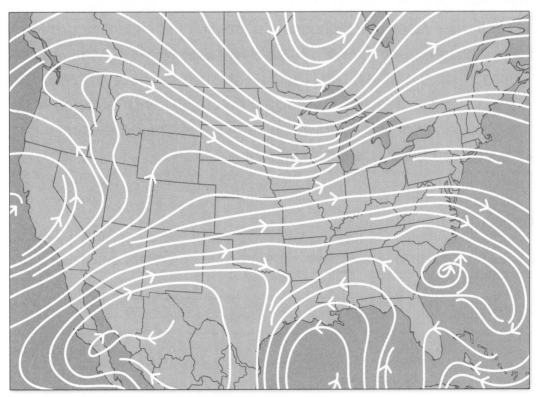

Example of a jetstream forecast

The World in Spatial Terms

Hurricanes and Typhoons

Define It!

typhoon: a hurricane-like storm in Southeast Asia or China

sustained: consistently at or above

catastrophic: causing sudden great damage

Hurricanes and typhoons are the largest storms on Earth. They are groups of thunderstorms clustered together in a huge swirling mass of air. In order to be classified as a hurricane or a typhoon, the storm needs to have sustained, or consistent, winds of over 74 miles per hour (119 kph). Hurricanes and typhoons are known for producing massive amounts of rain, flooding, and sometimes even tornadoes as they move over land.

A hurricane and a typhoon are the same thing. It just depends on their location. In the northwestern Pacific Ocean near Southeast Asia and China, the storms are called typhoons. In the Atlantic and northeastern Pacific Ocean, around the Caribbean Sea and off the coast of Mexico, they are called hurricanes. Hurricanes develop over oceans with water temperatures of 80°F (27°C) or higher. Maps are created to show these specific kinds of weather.

Both hurricanes and typhoons are rated for their intensity on the Saffir-Simpson Hurricane Wind Scale. They receive a 1 to 5 rating based on their sustained winds. The strongest of these storms is a Category 5 with wind speeds of over 157 miles per hour (253 kph). Catastrophic, or major, damage will occur from this type of storm. Once the storm hits land, it will gradually weaken and lose its intensity.

Answer the items.

1. Explain the difference between a hurricane and a typhoon.

   _____

   _____

2. Have you or someone you know witnessed this type of storm? If so, where and when?

   _____

The World in Spatial Terms

Giant hurricane
seen from space

2 PM Tue

2 PM Mon

2 AM Mon

2 PM Sun

2 AM Sun

Tropical Depression	Tropical Storm	Category 1	Category 2	Category 3	Category 4	Category 5
39 mph	39–73 mph	74–95 mph	96–110 mph	111–129 mph	130–156 mph	157+ mph

Circle shows possible storm center locations

Storms on Earth

Read the statement. Write *true* or *false*.

1. A meteorologist is someone who studies weather. _____

2. Hurricanes and typhoons are two very different kinds of storms. _____

3. Radar graphics show where rain is falling. _____

4. The atmosphere is the water on Earth. _____

5. Sustained winds are winds that are consistently at or higher than a certain speed. _____

6. The jet stream is the wind or air currents in the upper atmosphere. _____

7. Trade winds happen only at the North and South Poles. _____

8. Catastrophic damage from a storm means only a few small items were damaged. _____

Think About It

What type of storms occur where you live? Hurricanes, typhoons, tornadoes, thunderstorms? What type of storm seems most dangerous to you?

_____

_____

_____

_____

_____

The World in Spatial Terms

Weather Report

Map storm movement in your local area and project in which direction the storm is heading. Then give a weather report about it.

What You Need

- simple map of your local area
- colored pencils
- Internet access
- samples of severe storms radar maps and weather symbols

What You Do

1. Find a black-and-white print map of the town or city in which you live.

2. Research what radar and satellite maps look like when there is severe weather such as tornadoes, hurricanes, and thunderstorms. If you are using the Internet, start by typing in "hurricanes, thunderstorms on radar." The images you see may be a sample of what your finished map could look like.

3. Based on the storm images you saw on the Internet, use colored pencils on your map to draw a storm over your area. Note that reds and oranges are where the rain is heaviest, and may also be hail. Add in any other symbols you could include such as snow, tornadoes, and lightning.

4. Plot arrows on your map to show in which direction the storm is moving. Note that if it is a tornado in the United States, it is likely moving from the southwest to the northeast.

5. After your map is finished, show it to your family and give them a weather report about the storm and its movement.

The World in Spatial Terms

Skill:
Write informative text to convey information and experiences clearly

More Than Just Weather

Meteorologists study weather. But that could mean they need to know quite a few things in addition to weather. What expertise do you think a weathercaster needs to have about maps before he or she presents a weather report on television? Write to explain your thoughts.

_____

_____

_____

_____

_____

_____

_____

_____

_____

_____

_____

Skill Sharpeners: Geography • EMC 3746 • © Evan-Moor Corp.

The World in Spatial Terms

City Lights at Night

Concept:
Places and environments have spatial organization.

This summer I went to the Dark Sky Festival at Bryce Canyon National Park in Utah with my family. Southern Utah has incredibly dark skies. The area is pollution free and there aren't any cities nearby. That, combined with the high elevation of the area, make the views of the stars incredible. The rangers there said we would be able to see up to 7,500 stars at night.

Near the end of the festival, one of the presenters showed us a map of the world at night. On it we could clearly see city lights and where most of the world's population centers were. Of course, the East Coast and New York City were full of lights. I noticed many other brightly lit cities in the Northern Hemisphere, too, such as Chicago, Los Angeles, Phoenix, Boston, Miami, London, Paris, Rome, Tokyo, and Hong Kong. I also picked out Auckland, Sydney, Santiago, and Rio de Janeiro in the Southern Hemisphere—all by seeing their lights at night on the map.

I noticed a pattern as I looked at the night map. More people live near oceans than they do inland. And large cities tend to be clustered together. Then I found southern Utah, where I was at the time. There was hardly a light to be found. My family and I looked through telescopes, realizing that star gazing here was going to be much better than anything we'd experience at home.

The World in Spatial Terms

One Square Inch

The World in Spatial Terms

In a world of city lights and human noise, there are very few quiet places left. But there is at least one—a one-inch spot in Olympic National Park in Washington—possibly the quietest place in the United States. Quiet, in this case, is defined as no human noise at all. So, what do you hear instead? You hear crickets, frogs, birds, mosquitoes, water dripping, the river flowing in the distance, and footsteps of animals nearby in the forest.

The Hoh Rainforest section of the park where the one-inch spot is located is filled with trees, ferns, mosses, and many living things. The area is isolated but only about three hours away from the busy metropolitan area of Seattle. It is a short distance, but it seems like a world away.

So how do you get to this one-inch location? Drive to the Hoh Rainforest and park at the visitor center. Hike 3.2 miles (5.15 km) on the Hoh River Trail. At the 3.2 miles mark, look for a small red-colored stone placed on a moss-covered log. This is the spot. Many people also use global positioning system, or GPS technology, to find the location. Using GPS, the location is 47° 51.959N, 123° 52.221W. Type those numbers into your GPS device, and it will help guide you to the exact location!

Answer the items.

1. How do you think people first located the quietest place in the world?

_____

_____

2. Do you think you can stand 15 minutes of no human noise at all? Explain your answer.

_____

_____

A GPS device being used to find the exact position in the forest

Moss-covered trees in the Hoh Rainforest in Olympic National Park, Pacific Northwest

The World in Spatial Terms

15

Concept:
Places and environments have spatial organization.

The World in Spatial Terms

Aurora Borealis

Define It!

aurora borealis: colorful northern lights

light pollution: man-made lights

atmosphere: the air and other elements surrounding Earth

The aurora borealis, also called the northern lights, is an incredible display of moving colors in the upper part of Earth's atmosphere. The bright lights can be pink, green, yellow, orange, blue, violet, and even white. The phenomenon happens all year but is best seen in winter when there is less light pollution, or man-made lights, and crisp, clear cold nights.

Particles from the sun float about in space. Some enter the upper parts of Earth's atmosphere and are drawn toward the magnetic fields around the poles. As the particles pass through our atmosphere, they interact with oxygen, nitrogen, and other elements. The collision of these particles causes the lights. The color the aurora gives off depends on what elements the sun's particles collide with and at what altitude. If the main atmospheric element involved is oxygen, a greenish-yellow or red will be given off. If it is nitrogen, red, violet, and blue colors will be seen. The colors can also mix.

Since the poles are where the sun's particles are drawn, the best places to see the aurora borealis is in far northern latitudes. For example, prime locations include Alaska, northern Canada, Norway, Finland, and Sweden, which are all partially within the Arctic Circle. At times of high amounts of solar activity, the auroras can be seen farther south into England and Scotland, as well as in northern parts of the United States.

Answer the items.

1. Would you like to see the northern lights? If so, which country would you like to view them from? Explain your answer.

_____

2. How do human actions affect the visibility of the northern lights?

_____

Skill Sharpeners: Geography • EMC 3746 • © Evan-Moor Corp.

A beautiful green and red aurora dancing over the Jokulsarlon Lagoon, Iceland

Prime locations to view the northern lights

The World in Spatial Terms

Skill:
Identify content
vocabulary

The World in Spatial Terms

Special Places on Earth

Write the word or words next to its definition.

| aurora borealis | light pollution | metropolitan | atmosphere |
| oxygen | nitrogen | GPS | rainforest |

1. an element in the atmosphere that helps to create red, violet, and blue colors   _____

2. air and other elements blanketing the Earth   _____

3. the lights seen in winter in northern latitudes   _____

4. an element in Earth's atmosphere that helps create greenish-yellow and red colors   _____

5. a dense area of trees, mosses, and ferns   _____

6. densely populated city and surrounding communities   _____

7. a device used for finding exact locations   _____

8. man-made lights   _____

Think About It

Which would you want to go and see first: the one-inch spot, the aurora borealis, or the Dark Sky Festival? Tell why.

_____

_____

_____

Skill Sharpeners: Geography • EMC 3746 • © Evan-Moor Corp.

Skill:
Apply geography concepts in context

Your Own Quiet Spot

Locate and describe a quiet spot near where you live. Then direct someone to that exact spot without taking them there.

What You Need

- park or natural area near your home
- pencil
- paper and ruler
- journal
- small object

What You Do

1. With adult supervision, find the quietest spot near where you live. Go to that location.

2. In your journal, write all of the noises you hear over a 15-minute time span. Note if they are human noises or noises from nature.

3. After 15 minutes in this quiet spot, if you don't think it is quiet enough from human noise, find another location that is better. Repeat step 2 in the new location. Pick the spot that is the quietest.

4. Put a small, special object in the very quietest one-inch location in your quiet spot.

5. Create a map to the location. Write the directions beginning at your house. Include visual markers that will lead a person right to your one-inch location.

6. Give the directions to someone and see if he or she can follow your directions and find your quiet spot.

The World in Spatial Terms

Skill:
Write informative text to convey information and experiences clearly

Star Gazing

How can cities make sure that natural locations stay free of human light pollution so the night sky can be clearly seen and studied? Write to explain your ideas.

_____

_____

_____

_____

_____

_____

_____

_____

_____

_____

_____

_____

Skill Sharpeners: Geography • EMC 3746 • © Evan-Moor Corp.

Mexico City

My family and I just spent a month in Mexico City. Our relatives live in different places all around the city. They shared some of Mexico City's history with me.

Mexico City, or Ciudad de México, was built by the Aztecs on an island on Lake Texcoco in 1325. The city was originally called Tenochtitlán, but it was destroyed by a siege, or invasion, in 1521. Soon thereafter, Mexico City was built on the same spot, and it became the center of the Spanish empire. Eventually, the lake was drained and the city expanded. Now, hundreds of years later, Mexico City is one of the largest cities in the world with a population of over 21 million people!

Mexico City is in a basin, or valley, surrounded by tall mountains and volcanoes. One volcano, Popocatépetl, is active, and it is 17,877 feet (5,449 m) high. The city's elevation is around 7,350 feet (2,240 m). It took my family and I some time to get used to the altitude. Because the valley is surrounded by tall mountains, air pollution gets trapped there. My relatives told me that Mexico's people and government are finding ways to reduce the pollution.

When we weren't having our family gatherings, we often took the metro to see the sights. There were many museums, parks, gardens, and palaces to visit. We also saw archaeological ruins, ate great international food, and watched soccer games and bullfights.

© Evan-Moor Corp. • EMC 3746 • Skill Sharpeners: Geography

Concept:
There is a spatial organization to people on Earth's surface.

The World in Spatial Terms

Three Cities in Asia

Define It!

finances: business transactions

empire: territories or peoples under the rule of one government

estuary: an area where a river flows into the sea and is filled with fresh and salt water

trade: the action of buying and selling goods and services

Tokyo, Japan, is the most populated metropolitan area in the world. Founded in 1150, about 38 million people live there. Tokyo is also Japan's center of finances, or business and money transactions, as well as government. Nearly the whole population of Tokyo is Japanese, so it is a monoculture. Tokyo is known for having over 6,000 parks and gardens.

Delhi, India, is the second most populated city in the world. About 26 million people live in Delhi. It is one of the world's oldest cities, at almost 5,000 years old. The city is famous for its rickshaws. These three-wheeled, no-doored vehicles are used as taxis all over the city. New Delhi, the capital of India, was built by the British Empire. India gained independence from Great Britain in 1947.

The third most populated city in the world is Shanghai, China. There are about 24 million people living in Shanghai. It was built on an estuary of the Yangtze River. Shanghai is the trade center for China, which means that China sends its products to other countries and receives products from other countries. Shanghai is known for its towering skyscrapers and shopping districts with restaurants.

Answer the items.

1. Do you think there should be a limit on how many people can live within one city? Explain your answer.

_____

_____

2. Which of the three cities above would you want to visit first and why?

_____

The World in Spatial Terms

22

A population map of People's Republic of China

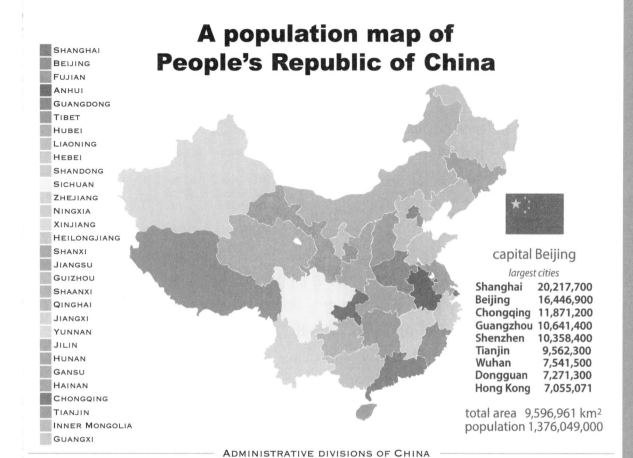

SHANGHAI
BEIJING
FUJIAN
ANHUI
GUANGDONG
TIBET
HUBEI
LIAONING
HEBEI
SHANDONG
SICHUAN
ZHEJIANG
NINGXIA
XINJIANG
HEILONGJIANG
SHANXI
JIANGSU
GUIZHOU
SHAANXI
QINGHAI
JIANGXI
YUNNAN
JILIN
HUNAN
GANSU
HAINAN
CHONGQING
TIANJIN
INNER MONGOLIA
GUANGXI

capital Beijing

largest cities

Shanghai	20,217,700
Beijing	16,446,900
Chongqing	11,871,200
Guangzhou	10,641,400
Shenzhen	10,358,400
Tianjin	9,562,300
Wuhan	7,541,500
Dongguan	7,271,300
Hong Kong	7,055,071

total area   9,596,961 km²
population 1,376,049,000

ADMINISTRATIVE DIVISIONS OF CHINA

Yuyuan Garden – a traditional shopping area in Shanghai, China

Not a Soul in Sight

Concept:
There is a spatial organization to people on Earth's surface.

The World in Spatial Terms

Define It!

alpine: high in the mountains

polar: near the North or South Poles

bacteria: microscopic one-celled organisms

permafrost: a frozen layer of soil beneath the topsoil

The three least populated regions on Earth are alpine zones, deserts, and polar areas. Alpine regions are high in the mountains. Another sparsely populated area is deserts. Some examples include the world's largest hot desert, the Sahara in Africa, and the world's driest desert, the Atacama in Chile. Polar regions are land-based areas near the poles. This includes the single least populated continent on Earth, Antarctica. The continent only has up to 4,000 part-time residents through the summer and about 1,000 over winter. There are no permanent citizens. Most of the continent is so harsh that it is devoid of, or absent of, life—even bacteria.

Sparsely populated polar climate areas outside of Antarctica are Northern Canada, Greenland, and Siberia. The soil in these regions has what is called permafrost, or a layer of soil that is frozen all year.

The least populated country in the world is the large island of Greenland. Greenland has over 836,000 square miles (over 2 million square kilometers) of land, but only a small population of about 56,000 people. That means in Greenland there is approximately one person per 15 square miles (40 square kilometers) of land.

Answer the items.

1. Do you think more people should try to live in places that have small populations? Explain your answer.

   _____

   _____

2. Considering the population, do you think there is a lot of pollution in Greenland? Explain your answer.

   _____

Skill Sharpeners: Geography • EMC 3746 • © Evan-Moor Corp.

Moon Valley in the Atacama Desert, Chile

Antarctica ice desert landscape

Kangaamiut village in Greenland

The World in Spatial Terms

Skill:
Demonstrate
understanding
of geography
concepts

Lots of People or Not?

Read the statement. Write *true* or *false*.

1. *Ciudad de México* is Spanish for Mexico City. _____

2. Trade means products that go to and from a country. _____

3. Finances are business and money transactions. _____

4. An empire is a group of cities working together. _____

5. An estuary is where a river and the sea meet that has both fresh water and salt water. _____

6. Alpine regions are in deserts. _____

7. Polar regions are located near the poles. _____

8. Permafrost is a layer of soil on top of the ground that is frozen. _____

9. Bacteria are microscopic multicelled organisms. _____

10. *Monoculture* means that several cultures share the area. _____

Think About It

Highly populated cities were deliberately built in specific locations. What do you think would make an area a likely place to hold a large population? What features would that area have to have?

_____

_____

_____

_____

The World in Spatial Terms

Skill Sharpeners: Geography • EMC 3746 • © Evan-Moor Corp.

I Want to Visit...

Create a slideshow of a place you read about in this unit.

Skill:
Apply geography concepts in context

What You Need

- Internet access
- computer software program to create and show text and pictures

Palacio de Bellas Artes (Palace of Fine Arts) – a famous theater, museum, and music venue in Mexico City

What You Do

1. Choose one of the locations you read about in this unit.

2. Use the Internet to research tourist attractions and areas of nature in that location.

3. Save pictures of the attractions you find. Write details about those areas, including their specific locations in the city or country.

4. Make a slideshow. Write captions that include the name of the attraction, where it is, what to do there, and its history.

5. If possible, add a map of the city or country and also a regional or world map showing its location.

6. Present your slideshow to your family and friends.

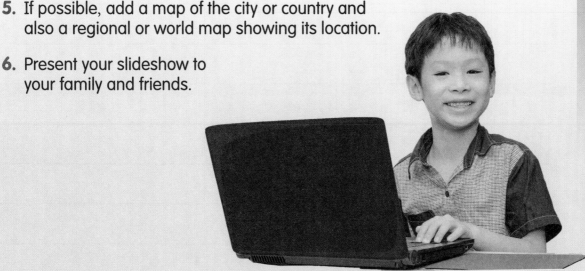

The World in Spatial Terms

Skill:
Write narrative text about real-world situations

Large City or Small Town?

Pretend you moved from a small town to a very large city. Write about how life is different for you. Include details about how the city looks, sounds, smells, and feels. Include the locations of the small town and the large city.

_____

_____

_____

_____

_____

_____

_____

_____

_____

_____

_____

_____

The World in Spatial Terms

28

Concept:
Places are locations having distinct characteristics.

We Won the Lottery!

Several months ago, we won the lottery. But we didn't receive any money. Instead, we were some of the lucky few who got to go inside a gigantic tomb in Ireland on the winter solstice. On the day of the event, we got lucky again—it was a rare sunny day.

Newgrange is a Neolithic tomb. *Neolithic* means it dates back to the Stone Age, which was a period of time when weapons and tools were made of polished stone, wood, bone, or horn.

I did say *tomb*. There are remains of people buried in it. The whole burial site is a gigantic mound shaped like a kidney. It is quite a popular site to visit, but especially on winter solstice.

Newgrange was built around 3200 BC. That means it is over 5,000 years old! The roof, made of rocks and sealed with capstone, is covered with grass and is still waterproof. Surrounding the tomb are 97 stones, many of which are decorated with ancient art. The best one is the entrance stone, full of swirling patterns.

There is a long passageway to the center where the event takes place. On December 21 every year, only 100 people are chosen by lottery to attend the event. At dawn on the shortest day of the year, sunlight enters the chamber through a narrow opening above the entrance. It lights up the whole room in a grand way. The people who built the tomb did this on purpose.

This isn't just for the light. The shortest day of the year celebrates nature's rebirth, promising renewed life to crops, animals, and humans.

Places and Regions

A Trip to Iceland

Concept:
Places are locations having distinct characteristics.

Define It!

hemispheres: the two halves of Earth

solstice: the turning point in winter or summer when days start to grow longer or shorter

orbit: to travel around

The winter solstice in the Northern Hemisphere is the shortest day of the year. But in the Southern Hemisphere, it is the longest day of the year. Hemispheres are the two halves of the Earth, divided at the equator. Solstice occurs two days each year when the sun is either at its highest or its lowest point in the sky.

Earth orbits around the sun once per year. Because Earth is tilted at an angle, the Northern or Southern Hemisphere is tilted toward the sun at different times of the year and is therefore closer to it. The Northern Hemisphere tilts toward the sun in summer and away from the sun in winter. The solstice marks the turning point when days start to grow longer in winter and shorter in summer.

Reykjavik is the capital of Iceland. It is the northernmost capital in the world at 64 degrees north latitude. That causes Reykjavik to get only about three hours of sunlight on the winter solstice and nearly 22 hours of sunlight on the summer solstice on June 21st. Because of the long, dark days of winter, residents adapt by spending more time indoors. When summer comes along, and it is light until late hours of the night, people in Iceland celebrate by staying outdoors! They also learn to sleep when it is light outside.

Answer the items.

1. Do you live in the Northern Hemisphere or the Southern Hemisphere?

   _____

2. At what time of the year where you live do the days grow longer? Do you like it? Why or why not?

   _____

   _____

   _____

Places and Regions

Skill Sharpeners: Geography • EMC 3746 • © Evan-Moor Corp.

Winter Solstice

(Western Hemisphere, December 21)

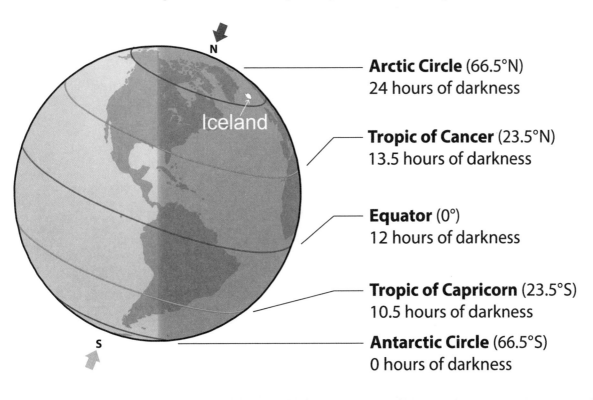

Arctic Circle (66.5°N)
24 hours of darkness

Tropic of Cancer (23.5°N)
13.5 hours of darkness

Equator (0°)
12 hours of darkness

Tropic of Capricorn (23.5°S)
10.5 hours of darkness

Antarctic Circle (66.5°S)
0 hours of darkness

Reykjavik, the capital city of Iceland

High-Elevation Capital

Define It!

plateau: a high-elevation flat land

latitude: a distance from the equator

climate: the year-round weather of an area

The capital of Ecuador, Quito, has the highest elevation of any capital city in the world. Quito sits on a plateau, or long stretch of high-elevation flat land, in the Andes Mountains of South America. The elevation of the city is 9,350 feet (2,850 m).

Quito is encircled by high mountains, several of which are volcanoes. Some of them are snowcapped, despite the city being located almost exactly on the equator. The most prominent of Quito's active volcanoes is Cotopaxi at 19,393 feet (5,911 m) elevation.

Quito is less than one degree south latitude from the equator. Quito's elevation, though, gives it a moderate climate (not too hot or cold) year-round and there are only two seasons—a wet season and a dry one.

Because Quito is almost exactly on the equator, the amount of hours of sunlight throughout the year hardly changes. The average amount of sunlight year-round is 12 hours. In fact, the longest day of the year in Quito is only one minute longer than the shortest day of the year! That is quite a contrast from Iceland and other places close to the poles.

Answer the items.

1. In your own words, describe the weather in Quito.

_____

_____

2. Would you prefer to live in a place with lots of seasonal weather changes or a place with hardly any weather changes?

_____

_____

Places and Regions

The volcano Cotopaxi in Quito, Ecuador, erupted in 2015.

The Middle of the World Monument in Quito, Ecuador, is visited by thousands of tourists.

Places and Regions

Skill:
Apply content vocabulary

How Much Sun?

Solve this crossword puzzle using words related to the sun.

| neolithic | stone age | solstice | hemispheres |
| latitude | plateau | tomb | orbit |

Across

2. period of time when weapons were made of polished stone, wood, bone, or horn
5. two halves of Earth
7. distance north or south of the equator

Down

1. longest and shortest days of the year
3. to go around something
4. dating back to the Stone Age
6. high-elevation flat area
8. burial place

Skill Sharpeners: Geography • EMC 3746 • © Evan-Moor Corp.

Places and Regions

Graphing Sunlight

Make a bar graph showing the number of daylight hours in your city.

What You Need

- Internet access
- pencil
- graph paper
- colored pencils

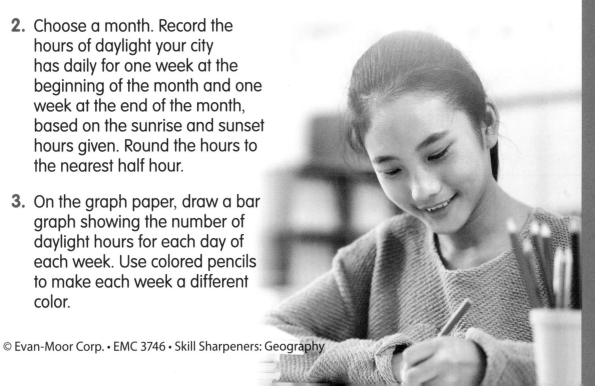

Example of one week.

What You Do

1. On the Internet, go to https://www.timeanddate.com/sun/ or another site with sunrise and sunset information, and type in the name of your city or the city nearest to you.

2. Choose a month. Record the hours of daylight your city has daily for one week at the beginning of the month and one week at the end of the month, based on the sunrise and sunset hours given. Round the hours to the nearest half hour.

3. On the graph paper, draw a bar graph showing the number of daylight hours for each day of each week. Use colored pencils to make each week a different color.

4. Give the graph a title.

5. Show the graph to your family and answer any questions they may have.

Places and Regions

Skill:
Write narrative text about real-world situations

A Letter Home

Using what you know about daylight hours around the globe, choose a place to live. Then write a letter home describing where you are, what the weather is like, and how you spend your time.

_____

_____

_____

_____

_____

_____

_____

_____

_____

Places and Regions

Skill Sharpeners: Geography • EMC 3746 • © Evan-Moor Corp.

Can You Keep a Secret?

Concept:
Places are locations having distinct characteristics.

Last summer my family and I drove up a long winding road high into the remote White Mountains of eastern California. Why did we go? To see the oldest living things on Earth—bristlecone pines.

Bristlecones live only at high elevations in the western parts of the United States. This includes only a very few places in California, Nevada, Utah, Arizona, New Mexico, and Colorado. The trees live in small groves usually above 9,000 feet elevation, where the conditions are harsh with extreme cold, high winds, and a short growing season. Because of this, scientists call them extremophiles.

We chose to go to the White Mountains to see what was said to be the oldest living tree in the world, Methuselah. Methuselah is named after the longest living person in the Bible. The tree is at least 4,848 years old, according to scientists who took core samples to determine its age. Rangers keep Methuselah's exact location a secret to protect it from possible vandals.

We circled around the grove, looking closely at the oldest and most gnarled trunks. We wondered which tree was Methuselah. At the end of the hike, we found out that another recently discovered tree is even older—over 5,000 years old!

Either way, visiting the bristlecones of the West is something I will never forget.

Places and Regions

Concept:
Places are
locations
having distinct
characteristics.

Three Great Trees

New Zealand is home to one of the world's most ancient trees called Kauri. They can live well over 2,000 years. Relatives of Kauri grew during the Jurassic period of dinosaurs from about 200 to 146 million years ago. Now the trees grow only in the north part of New Zealand's North Island.

Kauri trees grow to about 164 feet (50 m) tall. Their trunks make them the largest tree by volume in New Zealand. Some Kauri trunks are up to 52 feet (16 m) around, making them rival an even more massive tree in California, the giant sequoia.

Giant sequoias are the largest trees in the world. They grow close to 320 feet (97 m) tall and can live up to 3,000 years. The size of their trunk is what makes them so massive. The General Sherman tree is the largest sequoia, with a circumference of 102 feet (31 m) at its base! Sequoia trees live only in 75 groves in California's Sierra Nevada mountains. They dwell in an elevation range of 5,000 to 7,000 feet where there are snowy winters and warm, dry summers.

California also has another massive tree, the coastal redwood. Redwoods, a relative of the sequoia, live only along California's central and north coast and southern Oregon where they get a great deal of water from fog off the ocean. Coastal redwoods can reach 380 feet (116 m) tall, but because their trunks are thinner, they are not as massive as sequoias.

Answer the items.

1. There were other trees living 3,000 years ago. Why do you think the giant sequoias survived but the others didn't?

_____

_____

2. Why do you think California has two of the largest tree types in the world?

_____

Places and Regions

Tane Mahuta – largest
Kauri tree in Waipoua
Forest, New Zealand

General Sherman – largest
sequoia in Sequoia National
Park, California

Coastal redwood

Places and Regions

Upside-Down Tree

Concept:

Places are locations having distinct characteristics.

Define It!

tropical: warm, moist area near the equator

canopy: covering of leaves and branches

hollows: holes or depressions

treeline: elevation where trees can no longer grow

One of the oldest and most unusual trees in the world is the baobab tree. The nine species of this tree grow in the tropical and savanna regions of Africa, Madagascar, and Australia.

The most recognizable of the baobab trees have bottle-shaped trunks and very little canopy, or covering of branches and leaves. These trees can grow to 98 (30 m) feet tall, and their trunks can measure up to 36 feet (11 m) in diameter.

The flowers of the tree give off a sweet-and-sour smell that attracts bats and insects at night. The trunks have hollows in them, making them perfect homes for all kinds of creatures, including scorpions, lizards, birds, tree frogs, snakes, and squirrels. Native peoples used all parts of the baobab for shelter, food, and drink, as well as for making canoes and rope, among other things.

The tree line is the elevation at which trees can no longer grow due to cold, harsh weather and lack of water. Mt. Kilimanjaro is Africa's tallest peak at 19,340 feet (5,895 m) in elevation, and it is snowcapped despite being near the equator. The area around this mountain is forested with many trees including baobabs. Mt. Kilimanjaro's tree line is at 13,000 feet (3,962 m), and from there to the summit is mostly rocky, barren desert.

Answer the items.

1. Why do you think the baobab tree is described as being unusual?

   _____

   _____

2. Why can't baobab trees grow near the top of Mt. Kilimanjaro?

   _____

Places and Regions

Baobab trees near Morondava, Madagascar

Mt. Kilimanjaro from Amboseli National Park in Kenya, Africa

Places and Regions

Skill:
Use visual
discrimination

Where Are the Trees?

Find these words about trees in the word search.
Hint: Some are backwards.

baobab	kilimanjaro	tree line	methuselah
jurassic	sequoia	redwood	
extremophile	bristlecone	kauri	

c	i	s	s	a	r	u	j	l	d	g	e	w	k	b
u	h	n	v	g	q	p	s	o	u	l	y	g	i	b
x	c	i	n	r	t	d	o	g	i	j	i	p	l	m
b	h	r	e	l	z	w	p	h	z	m	h	a	i	h
f	r	q	c	n	d	i	p	q	e	y	v	i	m	l
v	l	p	r	e	i	o	v	t	f	z	u	o	a	a
l	d	v	r	k	m	l	h	c	c	n	d	u	n	s
a	q	f	l	e	h	u	e	t	g	k	j	q	j	d
k	t	b	r	i	s	t	l	e	c	o	n	e	a	g
z	a	t	z	e	j	b	u	y	r	p	j	s	r	c
q	x	u	l	b	a	o	b	a	b	t	t	k	o	w
e	v	a	r	x	w	y	n	m	p	q	h	v	q	k
h	h	b	t	i	a	w	f	u	r	a	s	p	n	t
y	e	o	s	b	v	n	h	k	y	d	s	n	r	u
m	d	b	d	g	w	j	e	m	i	r	n	y	q	r

Places and Regions

42

Skill Sharpeners: Geography • EMC 3746 • © Evan-Moor Corp.

Adopt a Tree

Skill:
Apply geography concepts in context

Adopt a tree for one year and record monthly details about it.

What You Need

- journal
- sketch pad
- colored pencils
- camera

What You Do

1. Pick a tree near you to study for a year or more.

2. Take pictures and draw sketches of the tree. Find out what type of tree it is and log it in the journal.

3. Record details about the tree. Write where the tree is located; how the leaves or needles look and feel and whether they change color and fall off; what the height and other measurements are; what animals, insects, or birds live in the tree; and any other observations you have.

4. Visit the tree once a month. Update your sketches and observations. Try to record even more observations about the tree. Does it flower or produce fruit? Has it changed due to weather-related events?

5. Take a new photo of the tree each time you visit it. Take new growth measurements if you can, too.

6. Regularly report your tree's status and information to your family.

The Most Unusual Trees

Many unusual trees grow in different places on Earth. Write to tell which of the trees on this page you would want to see first. Then explain why you think the tree is considered unusual and what elements in the environment may have contributed to its appearance.

_____

_____

_____

_____

_____

_____

_____

_____

Places and Regions

Ancient Gondwanaland

I just took a geography test and I think I did well. One question I know I got right is "How many continents are there on Earth?" There are seven of them: North America, South America, Asia, Europe, Africa, Antarctica, and Australia. Continents are the major landmasses on our planet, and they are always moving, drifting along Earth's surface.

One question the test did *not* ask is "How many continents did Earth use to have?" But I know the answer. About 600 million years ago, much of the land on Earth formed a major supercontinent called Gondwana, or Gondwanaland. Many of today's continents were joined together back then, including South America, Africa, Arabia, Madagascar, India, Australia, and Antarctica. This supercontinent can still be seen today by matching the puzzle-like shapes of the shorelines of western Africa and eastern South America.

The supercontinent was first assembled about one billion to 542 million years ago by plate collisions on the globe. About 300 million years ago, Gondwana collided with Laurasia, or what is now North America, Europe, and Siberia, to form Pangaea. Then about 200 million years ago, Gondwana and Laurasia finally began to drift apart. This started with Africa and South America separating. Later, Madagascar came apart from India. Then Australia drifted away from Antarctica. India then eventually collided with Eurasia about 45 million years ago, which formed the world's highest mountain range, the Himalayas.

When all these landmasses were together, they had similar climates, or weather. That led to the plants, animals, and organisms of the massive continents to be similar. The next time there is a geography test on the past, I will be ready!

LAURASIA & GONDWANA
120 million years ago

Reading

Concept:
The boundaries and characteristics of regions change.

A United Germany

Define It!

Cold War: a period of time when there was a fear of war between countries

diplomat: someone who represents a country

Tor auf: means "Open the gate" in German

When World War II ended, Germany was split into four territories in 1945. The eastern part went to the Soviet Union and the western parts went to the United States, Great Britain, and France.

Because of this new division, the city of Berlin, Germany, became West Berlin and East Berlin. Over the years, tensions flared up between the two sides. On August 13, 1961, the Soviet Union started to erect a 12-foot (3.7-m) wall of concrete to separate the sides. This caused thousands of people to quickly leave East Berlin.

Hostility continued to grow between the Soviet Union and the West. This led to a period of history called the Cold War, during which people feared a real war could break out between the two countries.

After the wall was finished, 12 checkpoint stations were set up. The most well-known of them was called Checkpoint Charlie, located in the center of Berlin. Only diplomats or other officials with proper papers could cross the border at a checkpoint.

Eventually, the Cold War ended, and on November 9, 1989, the Soviet Union said "Tor auf," meaning "Open the gate!" Over two million people crossed the border that weekend alone! In the end, on October 3, 1990, East Germany and West Germany were officially reunited.

Answer the item.

Why do you think so many people crossed between East and West Germany after the wall was taken down?

_____

_____

Places and Regions

Skill Sharpeners: Geography • EMC 3746 • © Evan-Moor Corp.

Map of Berlin
during the Cold War

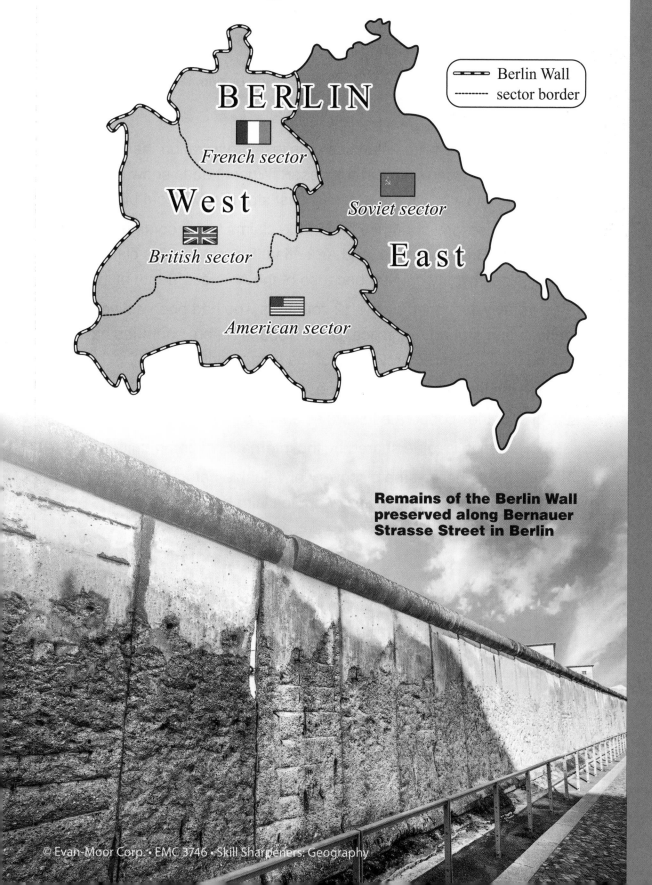

BERLIN

Berlin Wall
---------- sector border

French sector

West

Soviet sector

British sector

East

American sector

**Remains of the Berlin Wall
preserved along Bernauer
Strasse Street in Berlin**

Concept:
The boundaries and characteristics of regions change.

Places and Regions

Sharing a Continent

Antarctica is the coldest, windiest, and driest continent on Earth. The entire landmass also holds 90% of the world's ice in the form of glaciers. But actually, little moisture falls. Antarctica gets less precipitation than most of the Sahara, the world's largest hot desert. When it does snow in Antarctica, the snow blows like a desert dust storm in whiteout blizzards.

In the past, several countries had made claims to the continent, including Great Britain, France, and Argentina. But none of the claims were recognized by any country because of the Antarctic Treaty of 1959.

This treaty was signed by the 12 countries who had been active exploring in and around Antarctica. Since 1959, 41 more countries have signed the treaty. Specific provisions of the agreement include:

1. Use the land for peaceful purposes only.
2. All countries cooperate toward scientific exploration.
3. The science is to be shared by the international community.

Some experts believe the discovery of valuable natural resources in Antarctica could lead countries to want to claim land there again, but so far the treaty is still being followed.

Answer the items.

1. Why do you think 41 more countries have signed the Antarctic Treaty?

_____

_____

2. Do you think Antarctica should remain under the rules of the treaty?

_____

**Research station
in Antarctica**

**Port Lockroy, a British
research station on the
north-west shore of
Wiencke Island in the
Palmer Archipelago,
Antarctica**

Places and Regions

Managing Lands

Write the word next to its definition.

| Tor auf | diplomat | supercontinent | continent |
| Cold War | claim | treaty | resources |

1. when there was hostility between nations and a threat of war _____

2. an agreement between nations on how to use or share land _____

3. someone who works for a country _____

4. one of seven large landmasses on Earth _____

5. natural materials taken from Earth _____

6. means "Open the gate" in German _____

7. ancient continent of landmasses clumped together _____

8. when a country says it owns land _____

Think About It

What characteristics might a large tract of land have that would make countries want to claim it?

_____

_____

_____

_____

Places and Regions

Sign a Treaty

Skill:
Apply geography concepts in context

Find a special piece of land near you and write a treaty about the use of the land.

What You Need

- area of nature near where you live
- Internet access
- camera

What You Do

1. Choose a special piece of land using these criteria: land is near where you live, it is wild and not occupied by anyone, and it is public property or a park.

2. Take pictures of the land and write a list of reasons why the land should not be owned by a single person or managed in a private way.

3. Write a treaty for people to sign. Include pictures and a complete description and location of the tract of land you want protected. List the reasons why it should be protected. Design the treaty to look official. Add lines at the bottom for signatures.

4. Show the treaty to friends, families, and people who visit that area. Have them read it and sign it.

5. Thank the people who sign your treaty for participating in your activity.

Places and Regions

Changing Spaces

People change how they use different spaces all the time. For example, has your room always belonged to you, or was it your big brother's or sister's before it was yours? Has your family remodeled your house and changed the garage into a living room? Did your school build new classrooms or a new cafeteria or gymnasium? Write about a space that you know of that has changed.

_____

_____

_____

_____

_____

_____

_____

_____

_____

_____

_____

Places and Regions

Concept:
Physical processes shape features on Earth's surface.

Reporting from the Galápagos

I like to put together slideshows of my family's travels. I invited some friends over to show them the Galápagos Islands slideshow I made.

"We flew from Atlanta to Quito, Ecuador, which took a long time. But our journey wasn't over yet." I kept showing more slides as I continued the expedition to the archipelago, or group of islands, 600 miles or so off South America's western coast. *"It took us just an hour or so to fly to the airport on Baltra, one of the islands in the middle of the Pacific. From there, things got really interesting, really fast."*

I switched slides every few seconds. *"These are the amazing creatures we saw. I loved the playful sea lions. Some were up on shore barking away. Of course, we all took a short walk with the famous giant tortoises. They were so huge it was unreal! We also saw red Sally Lightfoot crabs walking sideways along the sand. There were birds everywhere, and my favorites were the Darwin's finches, named after Charles Darwin who studied wildlife on these very same islands. My favorite creatures, though, were the dinosaur-like marine iguanas basking on volcanic rocks near the ocean. It really was like being on a nature show. If you ever get a chance, I highly suggest that you also go to the Galápagos Islands!"*

I finished my slideshow and asked if there were any questions. There was only one: "Can we watch it again?"

Physical Systems

Colliding Plates

Define It!

introduced species: animals brought to an area by people

endemic: living nowhere else

tectonic plates: parts of the Earth's crust that move continuously

The Galápagos Islands are about 600 miles (966 km) off the coast of Ecuador. They consist of 13 major islands and many smaller ones. The Galápagos Islands are famous for their unusual wildlife. The animals that live there are classified into three categories. The first is native creatures that are natural to the islands but also live elsewhere. One example is the peregrine falcon. The second is introduced species, such as goats, that were brought to the islands by humans. The third and most prolific example of wildlife on the Galápagos Islands is its endemic species. These are creatures that live nowhere else in the world. The Galápagos giant tortoise is a well-known example of an endemic species. It is the largest living species of tortoise.

The Galápagos Islands were formed by the collision of tectonic plates. Tectonic plates are parts of the Earth's crust that are in constant motion. The Nazca Plate and the South American Plate meet at the Galápagos Islands and collide beneath the Pacific Ocean, which causes volcanic activity. Volcanoes created the islands and continue to do so today. There have been over 50 eruptions there in the last 200 years.

Answer the items.

1. What kinds of relationships do you think the endemic species and the introduced species have?

   _____

   _____

2. Have you ever seen a volcano or evidence of volcanic activity? If so, where?

   _____

   _____

Physical Systems

Skill Sharpeners: Geography • EMC 3746 • © Evan-Moor Corp.

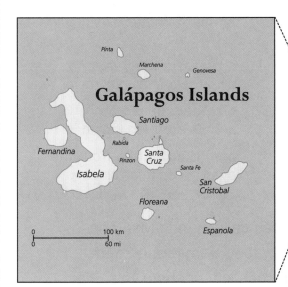

Galápagos Islands

Pinta
Marchena
Genovesa
Santiago
Rabida
Fernandina
Pinzón
Santa Cruz
Isabela
Santa Fe
San Cristobal
Floreana
Espanola

0   100 km
0   60 mi

PACIFIC OCEAN

ECUADOR

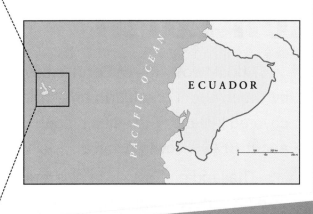

Peregrine falcon

Galápagos giant tortoise

**Wolf Volcano on Isabela
Island in the Galápagos**

Physical Systems

Concept:
Physical processes shape features on Earth's surface.

Landforms on Earth

Define It!

landform: a physical feature of the land

erosion: gradual wearing away of land by natural forces

archipelago: a group of islands clustered together

peninsula: land surrounded by water on three sides

About two-thirds of Earth is covered by water. About one-fourth of Earth is covered by land. The small amount left, about 10%, is covered in ice.

The land on Earth is in different shapes called landforms. These take on various shapes depending on how they were formed and how they have eroded due to wind, rain, frost, ice, or chemicals. Plate tectonics, or the collision of Earth's plates, also shapes the land.

Some of the major landforms on Earth include mountains, volcanoes, and mountain ranges. There are hills, which are more rounded and lower than mountains. There are valleys, which are formed between mountains and hills. Valleys often have rivers and tributaries, or smaller streams, running through them. There are plateaus, or high-elevation flat areas, and mesas, which are plateaus with steep sides. There are plains, which are large areas of flat land. Plains often have fertile soil good for growing crops. Islands are areas of land completely surrounded by water. They can be tiny or as large as a continent such as Australia. Groups of islands clustered together are called archipelagos. There are deserts with sparse vegetation. And there are peninsulas, or areas of land surrounded by water on three sides, such as Florida.

Answer the items.

1. Of all of Earth's landforms, which one describes the area where you live?

_____

2. What type of landform would you like to know more about? Explain your answer.

_____

_____

Physical Systems

Skill Sharpeners: Geography • EMC 3746 • © Evan-Moor Corp.

mountain range

valley

plateau

plain

archipelago

peninsula

Physical Systems

Skill:
Apply content
vocabulary

Places on Earth

Solve this crossword puzzle using words related to landforms.

archipelago	introduced	endemic	plates	plain
landform	erosion	tributary	mesa	peninsula

Across

2. smaller stream or river that feeds into a larger one
4. area of land that is surrounded by water on three sides
5. lives nowhere else
6. physical feature of the land
7. species of animals brought to an area by humans
9. Earth's crust that moves

Down

1. group of islands clustered together
3. flat area with steep sides
8. natural wearing away of land
9. large area of flat land

Skill Sharpeners: Geography • EMC 3746 • © Evan-Moor Corp.

Landform Maps

Create a continent that has a variety of landforms.

Skill:
Apply geography concepts in context

What You Need

- 11" x 17" (28 x 43 cm) sheet of white or light blue construction paper
- pencil
- colored pencils

What You Do

1. Draw a large continent on the construction paper. Leave room for a map key.

2. Think about the landforms you've learned about: mesa, plain, peninsula, archipelago, island, mountain, mountain range, volcano, valley with rivers and tributaries, desert, canyon, and others. Decide which landforms you will include in your continent.

3. In pencil, draw the landforms in different locations on your continent. Think about the relationships between landforms, such as mountains and valleys.

4. Create bodies of water such as seas or oceans around the land and label them.

5. Label each landform you included. Then color your map.

6. Add a map key.

7. Share your map with your family.

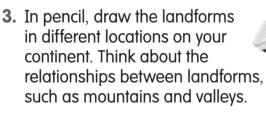

Physical Systems

Skill:
Write narrative text about real-world situations

New Landforms

Pretend a new landform appeared near where you live. What physical process caused it to be created? How did it change Earth's surface? Write a realistic fiction account of this event.

new landform

_____

_____

_____

_____

_____

_____

_____

_____

_____

_____

_____

_____

_____

Physical Systems

Skill Sharpeners: Geography • EMC 3746 • © Evan-Moor Corp.

Concept:
Climate shapes the characteristics of biomes.

Life in Death Valley

I just got back from a week of outdoor school. This year we went to Death Valley.

Death Valley is in southeast California in the middle of the desert. It got its name from people trying to cross it years ago—some didn't make it. Death Valley is one of the hottest places in the world, with temperatures reaching 130 degrees! At first glance, there doesn't appear to be many things living in the valley.

After five days there, I can say that there are many living things, including bighorn sheep, coyotes, bobcats, snakes, scorpions, chuckwallas (lizards), roadrunners, and my favorite, pupfish.

Death Valley is one of the few places in the world that pupfish live, and there are a few species there. Thousands of years ago, the valley was a lake and it supported the fish. But the climate dried and now only a few tiny spots house several hundred of these fish.

Pupfish are 1 to 2 inches (2.5 to 5 cm) long. They are silvery-gray to brown in color, and some males turn bright blue during mating season. These fish can survive in incredibly harsh conditions—water saltier than the ocean and water temperatures near freezing in winter to over 100 degrees in summer. Most other fish would die in those conditions.

If pupfish habitats are destroyed, there will not be any fish left. If people continue to pump water out of underground aquifers, the tiny pools pupfish are surviving in could dry up.

Physical Systems

Concept:
Climate shapes the characteristics of biomes.

Las Vegas, The Meadows

Define It!

oasis: a fertile green area in the desert

reservoir: a man-made lake

aquifer: an underground source of water

landscaping: altering the vegetation of land to use less water

The sprawling city of Las Vegas is about 120 miles (193 km) away from Death Valley. *Las Vegas* means "The Meadows" in Spanish. Before there was a city, the area had spring water that fed grasses that gave the city its name. It was an oasis in the desert—a fertile spot where water is found. Today, there are over two million people living in Las Vegas and tens of millions of tourists vacationing there each year.

Las Vegas is right in the middle of the Mojave Desert. It gets very little precipitation, yet the city keeps on growing. So how does it get water?

Hoover Dam was finished in 1936. It took 5 years for Lake Mead, the man-made lake, or reservoir, behind it to fill. Now, Lake Mead supplies 90% of Las Vegas's water, as well as some to Arizona and parts of California. But the lake is drying up and could be gone in the next five or so years. So what else can Las Vegas do for water? Up to 93% of the water in Las Vegas is treated and reused—hotels use recycled water in showers and sinks. Many people have received money from the city for converting their lawns to water-free landscaping. The city is also looking into using water from aquifers. But those aquifers provide springs and habitats for plants and animals, so this plan is controversial. For the time being, Las Vegas's water situation remains unresolved.

Answer the items.

1. Do you think Las Vegas should stop building more hotels and houses while they figure out a reliable water source? Explain your answer.

   _____

   _____

2. Is using an aquifer as a source of water a good idea? Why or why not?

   _____

Physical Systems

Skill Sharpeners: Geography • EMC 3746 • © Evan-Moor Corp.

Hotels, restaurants, and casinos in Las Vegas, Nevada

Hoover Dam

Physical Systems

63

Oasis in the Desert

Concept:
Climate shapes the characteristics of biomes.

Define It!

oasis: a place of plants and water in the middle of the desert

agua caliente: means "hot water" in Spanish

archaeological: related to studies of past civilizations

Just outside the Las Vegas city boundary is Red Rock Canyon Conservation Area. Red Rock Canyon is an area of towering red rock canyon walls. There are springs, waterfalls, and small pools of water— a little oasis in the desert. This area is home to wildlife such as the desert tortoise, bighorn sheep, and wild burro.

Agua Caliente Park is just outside Tucson, Arizona. *Agua caliente* means "hot water" in Spanish. There is archaeological evidence that shows people have been coming there for at least 5,000 years. The park has warm spring-fed waters, palm trees, and hiking trails.

In Israel, Ein Gedi is along the coast of the Dead Sea. People have been visiting this oasis for nearly 3,000 years. Today, the area is a nature reserve for the plants and animals that rely on the spring-fed waters.

Some say the world's most beautiful oasis is Chebika in Tunisia in northern Africa. It is called the Qasr el-Shams, which is Arabic for "castle of the sun." Several scenes from *Star Wars IV* were filmed there.

Answer the items.

1. Why do you think people, plants, and animals are drawn to an oasis?

_____

_____

2. Which of these oases would you like to go to first? Explain your answer.

_____

_____

Physical Systems

Waterfall in Ein Gedi Nature Reserve and National Park in Israel

Albino bighorn ram in Red Rock Canyon in Nevada

Mountain oasis Chebika in the Sahara Desert in Tunisia, Africa

Pond at Agua Caliente Park east of Tucson, Arizona

Physical Systems

65

Skill:
Demonstrate
understanding
of geography
concepts

Water Is Essential

Read the statement. Write *true* or *false*.

1. Pupfish live in many places around the world. _____

2. An oasis is a green area with plants and water in the desert. _____

3. Recycled water is water that is used one time. _____

4. An aquifer is an underground source of water. _____

5. *Aqua caliente* means "cool water." _____

6. Archaeologists are people who study the past. _____

7. A reserve is a special area that protects wildlife and plants. _____

8. A reservoir is a natural lake. _____

Think About It

If you were to find a spring in the desert that no one knew about, would you tell everyone or keep it a secret? Explain your answer.

_____

_____

_____

_____

_____

_____

Skill Sharpeners: Geography • EMC 3746 • © Evan-Moor Corp.

Physical Systems

Oasis Diorama

Create a miniature desert oasis.

What You Need

- disposable foil cooking pan
- small round pie tin
- blue waterproof paint or blue glass beads
- scissors or knife
- green plastic plants

- sand
- water
- plastic animals and people
- paintbrush
- rocks and pebbles

What You Do

1. Fill the tray two-thirds full with sand and spread it evenly.

2. Dig out a shallow area for your lake and place the pie tin in the hole.

3. Paint the inside of the pie tin blue for effect (or you may use blue glass oval beads.)

4. Place the plastic items around your diorama. They can be plants and trees, people, and animals. You may even want to make an artwork backdrop of mountains or sand areas behind the oasis. You can also add small rocks or pebbles to enhance your desert scene.

5. Fill the lake with water.

6. Share your display with others.

Physical Systems

Skill:
Write informative text to convey information and experiences clearly

A Very Rare Place

A desert oasis is a very rare place. It is a critical habitat for wildlife and essential for people living in and traveling through deserts. But some are in danger of disappearing. What do you think are the biggest threats to an oasis? Write about it.

_____

_____

_____

_____

_____

_____

_____

_____

_____

_____

_____

Physical Systems

Skill Sharpeners: Geography • EMC 3746 • © Evan-Moor Corp.

High-Altitude Superhumans

Concept:
There are multiple causes and effects of migration.

Last summer my parents and I climbed to the top of the highest mountain in the contiguous United States. Mt. Whitney in California is 14,505 feet (4,421 m) high. I had symptoms of altitude sickness the entire time I was above 10,000 feet (3,048 m). I moved slowly and felt sick, but I pressed on and summited. Now that I am turning 12 this summer, I am ready for more.

My mom told me about the Sherpas of Nepal. Sherpas live in the high altitudes of the Himalayas in Nepal, Tibet, Bhutan, and India. They have migrated to that region for centuries. After hundreds of years living far above sea level, Sherpas have become world famous for their ability to handle the ultra-high elevations.

The higher you go above sea level, the less oxygen there is. Near the summit of Everest, the world's highest mountain, there is about one-third the oxygen at sea level. Most people can't make that climb without canned oxygen, but Sherpas are often called superhumans at those high elevations.

Studies show that their system metabolizes, or uses, oxygen much more efficiently than most people, so their muscles respond faster in high-altitude conditions. The most famous Sherpa is Tenzing Norgay who was one of the first two people to reach the top of Everest at 29,029 feet (8,848 m) in 1953.

Many people use Sherpas as their guides on Himalayan high-altitude climbs. When I attempt to summit Everest, I want to have the best help, too.

EVEREST TEAM

Human Systems

Concept:
There are multiple causes and effects of migration.

Breathing at the Top of the World

Only a few groups of people have adapted to living at high elevations for extended periods of time. High elevations are considered areas over 13,000 feet (4,000 m).

High elevations have less oxygen in the air. People who climb to high altitudes may have symptoms of altitude sickness, or reduced oxygen, including headaches, vomiting, difficulty sleeping, impaired thinking, and the inability to keep active. These conditions are known as hypoxia. The best remedy is to go back downhill. At extreme elevations, a person can die from hypoxia.

Three groups of people called highlanders are known for being able to live at high elevations. The first are the people who live in the Andes Mountains of South America. They have adapted to the altitude because their bodies can carry more oxygen in each red blood cell than a normal person.

The next are the people of the Tibetan Plateau in the Himalayas in Asia. Their adaptation is that they breathe more often. The last are the Ethiopian highlanders in East Africa. They have also adapted, but the explanation for how they have adapted is still a mystery. One fact known about all three groups is that each generation who lives at a high altitude becomes better adapted to it.

Answer the items.

1. Why do you think each generation of people living at high altitudes becomes better adapted to it?

   _____

   _____

2. What is the highest elevation you have been at? Did you feel the effects of being at a higher elevation?

   _____

Human Systems

Skill Sharpeners: Geography • EMC 3746 • © Evan-Moor Corp.

Local farmer in the Andean highlands town of Tinqui, Cordillera Vilcanota ("mountain range"), Peru

Tibetan nomad with yaks walking across Shey La pass in the Himalayas, Nepal

Peiku Tso Lake at 15,062 feet (4,591 m) on the Tibetan Plateau

Human Systems

Concept:
There are multiple causes and effects of migration.

Desert Wanderers

Nomadic people move based on seasons, weather, and food sources. The Bedouin people are nomadic peoples of the Middle Eastern deserts. While most ancient peoples settled near a water source like a river, the Bedouin tribes or clans preferred the open desert. *Bedu* in Arabic means "One who lives in the open, in the desert." Bedouin people live in parts of Northern Africa, the Arabian Peninsula, Egypt, Israel, Iraq, Syria, and Jordan. They herd animals and migrate to the desert in winter months and move back to cultivated areas, or those farmed with crops, during summer.

The Bedouin have different animal species connected with their movements. Camel nomads are in the Sahara, Arabian, and Syrian Deserts. Sheep and goat nomads are in Jordan, Syria, and Iraq. Cattle nomads are in South Arabia and Sudan. It is estimated that there are about 4 to 5 million Bedouin people.

Modern Arabic states are not allowing Bedouin people to move about or graze animals as freely. Because of this, many Bedouin people are moving to the cities and taking modern jobs in government and the military.

Answer the items.

1. What do most nomadic tribes look for when they wander about?

   _____

   _____

2. If you were to lead a nomadic lifestyle, where would you like to roam and why?

   _____

   _____

Human Systems

Bedouin camp in the desert of Wadi Rum, Jordan, Middle East

Caravan of Bedouins and camels in sand dunes

Human Systems

Skill:
Identify content
vocabulary

Nomadic People

Match the definition to its word.

1. name for a person who lives at
   high elevations   •   • Sherpa

2. term for a group of people who
   move from place to place   •   • hypoxia

3. medical issue for those suffering   •   • highlander
   from lack of oxygen

4. area that is farmed for crops   •   • adaptation

5. name of a guide famous for being •
   able to withstand high elevations   • nomadic

6. when people have acquired traits •
   that help them survive   • cultivated

Think About It

If you lived with a nomadic group of people, what modern items
would you miss the most? Or, could a nomadic group have all the
amenities of a modern society?

_____

_____

_____

_____

_____

Human Systems

Skill Sharpeners: Geography • EMC 3746 • © Evan-Moor Corp.

A Day in the Life

Imagine that you are on a nomadic expedition, recording each day's events.

Skill:
Apply geography concepts

What You Need

- journal or paper
- Internet access
- pen or pencil

What You Do

1. Decide if you will pretend to be on a journey with a nomadic tribe that lives in a high-elevation mountainous area or a desert area.

2. Use the Internet to research more about the daily lives of that type of nomadic tribe.

3. Then go to a quiet space and imagine your life with that tribe. Next, record the happenings for one week in your journal.

4. Begin each entry with the date and time. Write about meals, significant events and hardships, dangerous conditions that were encountered, supply needs, and the amazing things you experienced.

5. Share your journal entries with your family.

Human Systems

Skill:
Write informative text to convey information and experiences clearly

Choose Your Life

Which nomadic lifestyle do you think is attainable for you: trekking and living at high elevations or in the desert? What would be easy parts of that life for you to adjust to? What would be more difficult? Realistically, do you think you could adapt to a nomadic lifestyle? Choose the life you think would be best for you and write about it.

_____

_____

_____

_____

_____

_____

_____

_____

_____

_____

_____

_____

_____

Human Systems

Skill Sharpeners: Geography • EMC 3746 • © Evan-Moor Corp.

My Irish Roots

Concept:
Migration shapes the cultural and physical landscape of places and regions.

Last summer I learned about my Irish roots, and it made the Statue of Liberty even more important to me. The statue towers over New York harbor. It is a symbol of freedom for those immigrating to the United States. A poem is inscribed on the statue's pedestal. It reads in part "Give me your tired, your poor, your huddled masses yearning to be free."

My great-grandma left Ireland at 18 years old. The year was 1907. At the time, Ireland was facing immense poverty and disease. My great-grandma came to the U.S. hoping for a better opportunity. She was on a steamship called *Red Star.* Other people on her ship came from Germany, Scandinavia, and other places in Europe. The journey across the Atlantic Ocean took two weeks. There were first- and second-class passengers onboard who were treated very well. Inspections of those passengers were done aboard the ship. But third-class passengers, called steerage passengers, were treated very differently. They spent the journey in cramped quarters near the bottom of the ship, seasick most of the time. That's where my great-grandma was.

After arriving in New York, third-class passengers were ferried over to Ellis Island, the checkpoint station for getting into the country. Inspections lasted from 3 to 5 hours. Doctors looked over the passengers and did what was called a "six-second physical." They looked for signs of any contagious diseases or ailments. Most people made it through, as did my great-grandma. She walked into the United States in 1907 and began a new life here without knowing anyone.

Immigrants waiting to be examined by doctors on Ellis Island, circa 1902

Human Systems

Angel Island

Human Systems

Define It!

interrogated: questioned in a forceful way

laborer: a person doing manual work requiring bodily strength

Angel Island is located in the San Francisco Bay in California. Coastal Miwok Native Americans used the island some 3,000 years ago as a fishing and hunting site. They left the shores of San Francisco and went there because the San Francisco mainland was becoming populated with people. Later, Spanish explorers established a cattle ranch on the island. Then it became a U.S. Army post. But the island is best known for being an immigration station.

From 1910 through 1940, about 175,000 Chinese immigrants came to the United States through Angel Island. However, it was not an easy process for them. Angel Island Immigration Station was known as "The Guardian of the Western Gate." It protected against unwelcome immigrants, rather than welcoming all. Many interrogations took place at Angel Island. The Chinese were often asked questions that were obscure, or difficult to understand and answer. Many Chinese people were kept for extended periods of time in detention barracks where families had to live separately—the men in one and the women and children in another. There, the Chinese scratched poems and messages about their hardships into the walls.

Despite the challenges, many Chinese made it into the U.S. They worked as laborers, farming, mining, and building railroads. Today, Chinese citizens live all over the United States, and they are an important part of American culture.

Answer the items.

1. How did Angel Island's landscape change over time?

_____

_____

2. Why did Angel Island's landscape change over time?

_____

_____

Skill Sharpeners: Geography • EMC 3746 • © Evan-Moor Corp.

Detained Chinese immigrants carved poems into the wooden walls of the detention barracks.

Angel Island Immigration Detention Center

Angel Island

Human Systems

Concept:
Migration shapes the cultural and physical landscape of places and regions.

Shelter in Europe

People from Africa, the Middle East, and southern Asia are pouring into Europe. They mainly come through Greece and Italy, as these countries are closer to the Mediterranean Basin where the immigrants are from. Some of the immigrants are crossing the borders illegally, and border patrols in Europe are tightening their security.

Refugees, such as people from Syria and Afghanistan, are fleeing war. Those from Eritrea, a small country in Africa, are escaping forced labor.

Many of these immigrants are housed in camps, and some are placed in detention centers. Most of these facilities are overcrowded and do not have enough resources to provide the immigrants with basic necessities.

As immigrants and migrants enter European countries, some people worry that there are not enough jobs available to support them. Some people don't want the immigrants to live there. Conversely, some people are working hard to help them start a new life.

Immigration and migration are ongoing challenging issues for many countries.

Answer the item.

Do you think all people fleeing wars and poverty should be allowed to go to new countries and start a new life?

_____

_____

_____

Human Systems

Syrian (Kurdish) refugee camp in Suruc, Turkey

Refugees from Ethiopia, Africa

Refugees trekking through Slovenia in the direction of Germany

Human Systems

Skill:
Identify content
vocabulary

Immigration

Write the word next to its definition.

steerage	immigrant	laborer	interrogate
refugee	migrant	detention center	

1. a person who moves from one place to another _____

2. a person who leaves a place to seek a way out of poverty _____

3. to question a person in a forceful way _____

4. the name given to third-class passengers _____

5. a person who leaves a place to escape war or dangerous conditions _____

6. a place where people are held before entering a country _____

7. a person who performs hard work _____

Think About It

Would you and your family ever consider leaving the country you are living in now? Is immigrating to another country possibly part of your future? Explain your answer.

_____

_____

_____

_____

Skill Sharpeners: Geography • EMC 3746 • © Evan-Moor Corp.

Human Systems

Family History Maps

Interview your family to find out where your ancestors are from. Then use a map to show your family's history.

Skill:
Apply geography concepts

What You Need

- world map
- pins or tacks
- scissors
- pencil and paper
- interviews with family members
- colored yarn
- sticky notes

What You Do

1. Interview the elders in your family. For example, grandparents, parents, aunts, and uncles. Ask if any of them were originally from another country. Document where two or more of your family members used to live and how they traveled to the country in which they currently live.

2. Plot the information you gather on the map. Use yarn and pins to mark the key points in each family member's journey. Place a sticky note at each location he or she stopped and write what he or she did while there.

3. Once you have finished the map, show your family and explain how it documents your family members' journeys.

Human Systems

Skill:
Write narrative text about real-world situations

A Long Journey

Write a story about a person who immigrated to another country. Tell why he or she needed or wanted to leave his or her homeland, and give a detailed account of his or her journey.

_____

_____

_____

_____

_____

_____

_____

_____

_____

Human Systems

Holiday Panic

Concept:
Economic systems of countries and regions consist of multiple coordinated activities.

I come from a gift-giving family. This generosity extends around the world. Some of my cousins live in Auckland, New Zealand, and others live in London in the United Kingdom. One year we were visiting my cousins in Auckland for the holiday season. My cousin Lori and I were texting our cousin Travis in London, and I let it slip that my mom hadn't mailed their gifts yet.

The gifts they sent us from London arrived on December 20. But in the midst of all our holiday shopping, it was almost Christmas by the time we sent them their gifts.

We shipped the packages out the morning of December 21. The postal clerk assured us that they were guaranteed to arrive at my cousin's door, halfway around the world, on December 24. I was relieved to know that the gifts would make it in time! However, it wasn't cheap. It cost my parents roughly $200.00 New Zealand dollars to ship the presents. That is about £110 British pounds, the money they use in London. My mom pointed out that it cost us more money to send the gifts than it did to buy them. Dad added, "True, but it is the thought that counts." Then I added, "They can always return the gifts in the UK and use the money!" We all laughed.

Human Systems

The Euro

Concept:
Economic systems of countries and regions consist of multiple coordinated activities.

Define It!

currency: a system of money used by a country

euro: currency used by 19 European countries

exchange rate: the amount of money received when exchanging one form of money for another

There are 195 countries in the world and 180 currencies. Some countries share their monetary systems.

For example, the 50 countries that make up Europe use 28 currencies. Some European countries, including Denmark, Norway, Sweden, Poland, Switzerland, and the United Kingdom, use their own currency.

On January 1, 1999, a group of Western European nations adopted a common currency called the euro. This monetary system is shared by 19 European countries, including Austria, Belgium, France, Germany, Greece, Italy, Portugal, and Spain. Why did they adopt a common currency? Doing so makes it easier for people to travel and purchase goods throughout these nations. The euro does not have to be exchanged from one country to the next in those 19 countries, so no exchange rate is needed. Now people in Europe can use the same money from country to country. Some people believe that using a common currency saves businesses and families time and makes it easier to budget for expenses. Others are not in favor of having a common currency.

Either way, the euro is the second most-traded currency in the world after the United States' dollar.

Answer the items.

1. Why are there fewer currencies than countries in the world?

   _____

2. Do you think it is a good idea to use different currencies in different countries? Why or why not?

   _____

   _____

   _____

Human Systems

The countries in green use a common currency, the euro.

Human Systems

A Barrel of Oil

Concept:
Economic systems of countries and regions consist of multiple coordinated activities.

Define It!

petroleum: another word for oil

plankton: tiny creatures in the ocean

fluctuate: to change or vary day by day

Oil is like currency. It has value and is used all over the globe. Oil is also called petroleum, which in Latin means "rock oil." Over millions of years, tiny aquatic creatures such as plankton float in the ocean, die, and then sink to the bottom. They get covered in mud and then eventually turn into oil.

Most oil is taken from the Earth by drilling wells. Pressure can also be used to bring oil to the surface. After oil is processed, it is shipped around the world in large tankers. Oil is used for heating and electricity, making asphalt and roads, and as fuel for cars, boats, and planes.

About 80 million barrels of oil are processed in the world each day. A barrel equals about 42 gallons (159 L). Some of the top oil producing countries of the world include Iran, the United States, and Russia. Saudi Arabia produces the most oil, making almost 12 million barrels a day.

Oil prices per barrel fluctuate based on supply and demand. The more oil is needed, the higher the price usually gets. Some countries make a set price agreement ahead of time so they can purchase oil without the price fluctuating.

Answer the items.

1. What do you think would happen if people were *not* able to get oil from the Earth?

   _____

   _____

2. What do you think causes the demand for oil to fluctuate?

   _____

   _____

Human Systems

Oil stored in barrels

Pacific Ocean offshore oil drilling rig off Southern California

Oil pump jacks on an oil field

Human Systems

Skill:
Apply content
vocabulary

World Currency

Solve this crossword puzzle using words related to currency.

| euro | currency | exchange rate | petroleum |
| oil | fluctuate | plankton | |

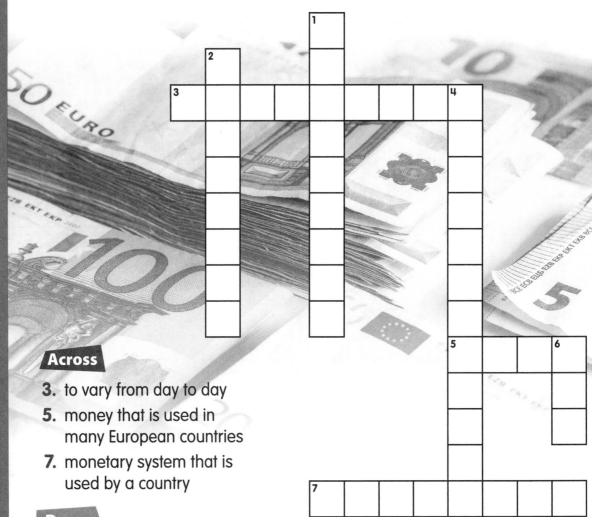

Across

3. to vary from day to day
5. money that is used in many European countries
7. monetary system that is used by a country

Down

1. another word for *oil*
2. tiny ocean creatures
4. amount of money a person receives when exchanging one type of money for another
6. natural substance used for heat, electricity, and fuel

Skill Sharpeners: Geography • EMC 3746 • © Evan-Moor Corp.

Human Systems

Exchanging Money

Skill:
Apply geography concepts in context

Plan a vacation and exchange money from one country to another using the current exchange rates.

What You Need

- world map
- Internet access
- paper and pencil
- highlighter

What You Do

1. Using the world map, choose five countries to travel to and highlight their locations.

2. Budget $500 U.S. dollars, euros, or whatever form of currency you use for each country you will visit.

3. Look up the currency exchange rates online at https://www.oanda.com/currency/converter/

4. Note how much money you will have according to the exchange rate in each country. Also note the kinds of currency you exchanged. For example, dollars to pounds.

5. Make a list of what your expenditures will be in each country. For example, hotel, food, transportation, and tourist destinations you will visit. Calculate the amount of money you will need for your trip.

Human Systems

Other Currencies

Money is used worldwide as currency. Oil is also used across the globe. Can you think of another item that has universal value that some people might accept instead of money? Write about it.

_____

_____

_____

_____

_____

_____

_____

_____

_____

_____

_____

_____

_____

Human Systems

I Am Roald Amundsen

Concept:
People cooperate to manage and use Earth's surface.

I put on my thick fur clothes, stepped into my padded winter boots, and walked in front of the audience.

"Hi!" I announced. "My name is Roald Amundsen. I am a Norwegian explorer of polar regions from the early 1900s. I am most famous for being the first person to lead a crew to the South Pole. My crew and I departed for the South Pole in October of 1911. It was almost summer in the Southern Hemisphere, and we needed to arrive at the South Pole at peak sunlight and during the warm season. The people on my team were Norwegians. We were racing against a British team to see who could reach the South Pole first.

"We used dog sleds to carry our gear and sometimes moved on skis. That helped us travel quickly through the snow. It took us almost two months to get to exactly 90 degrees south latitude. We took careful measurements using the angle of the sun and sextant readings to find the precise South Pole. Once we were there, we placed our Norwegian flag on the spot. We never saw the British team.

"Later, we learned that sadly they had all perished on their return journey. They were found frozen in their sleeping bags. The main reason was improper gear, and they had used ponies as their main method of transport."

As I ended my presentation, I gave my audience a final statement. "Now there is a permanent scientific research station at the South Pole that bears Amundsen's name as well as Scott's, the leader of the British party."

A Special Lake

Concept:
People cooperate to manage and use Earth's surface.

Define It!

flora: the plants of an area

fauna: the animals of an area

endemic: found nowhere else on Earth

UNESCO stands for United Nations Educational, Scientific, and Cultural Organization. Created in 1945, UNESCO's mission is to build peace, eliminate poverty, and create intercultural cooperation and partnerships through education, the sciences, culture, communication, and information. Part of UNESCO's mission is to bring nations together to protect and preserve some of the world's most special places. There are currently about 1,073 UNESCO World Heritage sites.

One such place is Lake Baikal in Siberia, Russia, the oldest lake in the world. Siberia is a vast area in south-central Russia. At 61 degrees north latitude, it is mostly cold, frozen, grassland known as tundra. Siberia is bordered by China and Mongolia, as well as by the Arctic Ocean to the north.

Lake Baikal is the largest freshwater lake in the world. It is 395 miles (636 km) long and up to 50 miles (80 km) wide. The lake is also the world's deepest at 5,315 feet (1,620 m). This huge lake is most famous for its unique flora and fauna, the majority of which are endemic, meaning they do not live anywhere else in the world. The area is home to a wide range of wildlife, including lemmings, brown bears, lynx, Siberian roe deer, wolves, and wild boar. Perhaps the most interesting mammal species found there is the nerpa, one of the world's only seals that lives entirely in freshwater.

Answer the items.

1. Do you think it is important for nations to work together to preserve places? Explain your answer.

_____

_____

2. Why do you think some of Lake Baikal's plants and animals are endemic?

_____

_____

Human Systems

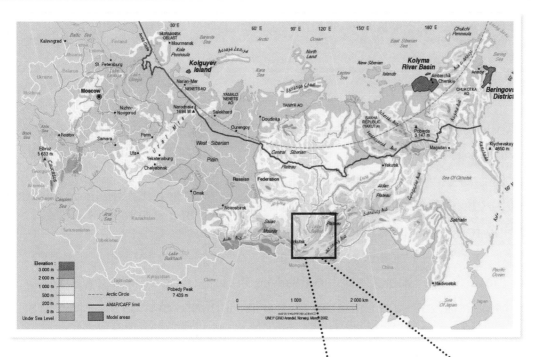

Baikal seal, or nerpa

Lake Baikal

Human Systems

Concept:

People cooperate to manage and use Earth's surface.

Who Owns the Oceans?

Define It!

canal: a man-made waterway for boats and ships

strait: a narrow area of water connecting two larger bodies of water

commodities: raw materials or agricultural products that are bought and sold

continental shelf: an offshore part of a continent in shallow water

About 70% of Earth is water, most of which is in the oceans. Large ships, barges, and tankers sail the oceans to transport products all over the world. Major shipping routes connect North America, Europe, and Asia Pacific. These routes pass through the Suez Canal in the Middle East, the Strait of Malacca near Malaysia, and the Panama Canal in Central America. The world's busiest route, or lane, is the Dover Strait in the English Channel. It is bordered by the United Kingdom and France. Over 500 ships a day pass through this narrow strait. Cargoes include oil from the Middle East to European ports and various commodities from North and South America to European customers.

As determined by the United Nations, countries have a right to what is called territorial waters offshore. The nearest country has control of the shipping lane offshore as long as it is still part of the continental shelf. The United Nations also states that a country's border can extend as far as 12 nautical miles (22 km) out to sea. Past that point, no country has territorial rights. Ships are allowed to travel within another country's territory in the ocean, as long as that country does not see it as a threat.

Human Systems

Answer the item.

Does the explanation of territorial waters offshore answer the question that the title of the article asks?

_____

_____

_____

_____

Skill Sharpeners: Geography • EMC 3746 • © Evan-Moor Corp.

This world map shows common shipping lanes used to transport goods across the world.

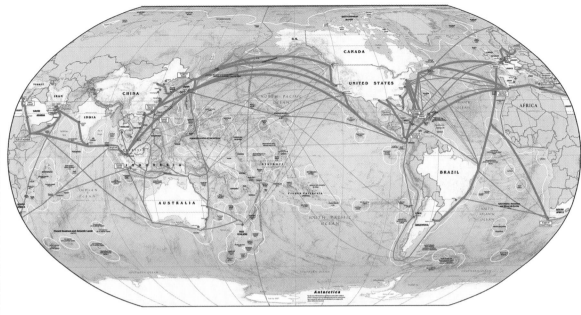

▬▬▬▬▬ Shipping lane
(line weight indicates significance of route, not volume of traffic)

Container ship under the Golden Gate Bridge in San Francisco, California

Human Systems

Skill:
Identify content
vocabulary

By Land or By Sea?

Write the word next to its definition.

UNESCO	tundra	flora	fauna
endemic	canal	strait	continental shelf

1. the animals of an area _____

2. a man-made waterway for ships _____

3. a frozen grassland _____

4. a narrow area of water connecting larger
   bodies of water _____

5. a group that helps preserve the world's
   special places _____

6. the plants of an area _____

7. living only in that area _____

8. a part of a continent in shallow water _____

Think About It

Would you like to explore a special place in the world? Do you
have an idea of where it may be? Why would you choose to go
to that place?

_____

_____

_____

_____

Human Systems

UNESCO World Heritage Sites

Skill:
Apply geography concepts

Write about UNESCO World Heritage sites, and then give a presentation to your family and friends.

What You Need

- Internet access
- computer software program to show text and pictures

Google

What You Do

1. Go to the links below to learn about UNESCO World Heritage sites.

   http://whc.unesco.org/en/interactive-map/

   http://whc.unesco.org/en/list/

2. Choose one or two sites to write about. Decide if you will write in a word processing program or create a PowerPoint® presentation.

3. Include information such as the name of the site and when it became one, the country in which the site is located, a description of the site, and photos.

4. Explain in your own words why you feel the site or sites you chose are important World Heritage sites.

5. Give a presentation to your family and friends based on the information in your report. Make sure that you have a good understanding of UNESCO's mission before you begin your presentation.

Floating village and rock islands in Halong Bay, Vietnam, Southeast Asia – a UNESCO World Heritage Site

Human Systems

Skill:
Write informative text to convey information and experiences clearly

A Protected Place Near You

Is there a large area of land or water near you that is protected? What is special about it? If it isn't protected, should it be? Write to answer these questions and give your opinions.

_____

_____

_____

_____

_____

_____

_____

_____

_____

_____

_____

Concept:
Human actions modify the physical environment.

My First Scuba Dive

When my family and I were visiting Australia, we saw one of the most amazing places on Earth, the Great Barrier Reef. On the last day of our vacation, we booked a tour to scuba dive.

The boat picked us up in the port city of Cairns. We went out to what seemed like the middle of the ocean. When I looked over the edge of the boat, I could see a kaleidoscope of colors in the water below us. We donned our gear, and the guides gave us last-minute instructions. Soon, my parents and I plopped ourselves over the side of the boat into the water. Once I got myself adjusted, I looked around underwater. I felt like I had entered a magical kingdom.

The Great Barrier Reef is a rainbow of colors. Our guides led us through mazes of coral, which is made from the skeletons of marine organisms, and schools of darting multicolored fish. The guides pointed to several reef sharks in the distance. We also saw sea turtles swimming about and a giant clam right below us. It was all very surreal and pretty amazing.

But suddenly, we entered a zone where the coral was no longer beautiful—it had a dull white and murky-brown color. After we finished our dive and climbed aboard the boat, we asked what happened to the coral. Our guides told us what was going on. Warmer sea temperatures from climate change were killing off parts of the reef. I was shocked and sad, realizing that what people do on Earth affects everything.

Environment and Society

A City Built on Water

Concept:
Human actions modify the physical environment.

Environment and Society

Define It!

sea level: the level of the sea's surface

canal: a waterway for transportation

gondola: a flat-bottomed boat with a high point at each end

Located in Northern Italy, Venice is constructed like no other city in the world. Known as the "City of Water," Venice is actually situated on a series of 118 islands. Because the city is right at sea level, canals were built as a means of transportation.

Venice's canals were first constructed as far back as AD 400. At that time, they were used for transporting goods throughout the city. Today, there are about 170 canals and over 400 bridges within Venice. They are still used for transportation of goods, as well as commuter thoroughfares for locals. In addition, millions of tourists come from all over the world to experience Venice's sights from the canals and bridges. The most important canal is the Grand Canal. It cuts the city in half and is used by water buses and taxis. Homes, apartments, and restaurants border both sides of the canals, making the city very picturesque. Venice also has many gondolas, which are boats used as water taxis, and they are quite popular with tourists. A trip to Venice is truly a unique experience.

However, Venice is slowly sinking, so the city floods frequently. Climate change may add to this with rising sea levels due to melting ice.

Answer the item.

Describe how human actions have modified the islands of Venice.

_____

_____

_____

_____

_____

Skill Sharpeners: Geography • EMC 3746 • © Evan-Moor Corp.

View of the Rio Marin Canal

Gondola near the Rialto Bridge, one of four that cross the Grand Canal

Grand Canal at sunset

Environment and Society

Concept:
Human actions modify the physical environment.

More Water Needed!

The world's population is currently over 7.6 billion. With so many people on Earth, there is a need for more water. One way to get more water is to seed clouds.

Cloud seeding increases the amount of rain that storms produce. It is done primarily in areas where there are droughts. It is also done in locations where extra rain can be stored in reservoirs for times when there is little or no rainfall. China, the United States, and Australia are three countries known to use cloud seeding regularly, but it is also used elsewhere.

When there are storm clouds, a chemical called silver iodide is released into the clouds by planes or from the ground. The particles are similar to ice crystals. This makes water droplets in the clouds cling to the particles and become heavier, causing them to fall out of the clouds as rain or snow, or precipitation.

Cloud seeding can increase rainfall by about 10 to 20%. This means a place that gets around 20 inches (51 cm) of rain per year can increase its rainfall to 22 to 24 inches (56 to 61 cm). Over large areas and long periods of time, cloud seeding can help places that are dry get enough water.

Answer the item.

Do you think cloud seeding should be done more often or less often? Explain your answer.

_____

_____

_____

_____

This wing rack holds burn-in-place silver iodide flares used for cloud seeding.

This rack of 102 ejectable silver iodide flares will be mounted on the belly of a plane.

A cloud combined with silver iodide produces rain.

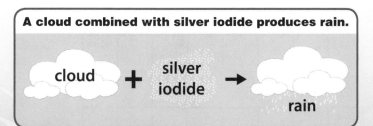

cloud + silver iodide → rain

Environment and Society

Skill:
Apply content
vocabulary

Dealing with Water

Solve this crossword puzzle using words related to water.

coral	climate change	sea level
gondola	cloud seed	precipitation
canal	reservoir	drought

Across

1. long period of dry weather
3. warmer temperatures now on Earth
6. rain, snow, sleet, or hail
7. hard material made from skeletons of marine organisms
8. man-made lake for storing water
9. waterway used for transportation

Down

2. special boat used as a taxi
4. to add chemicals to clouds to cause them to produce more precipitation
5. level of the ocean

Environment and Society

Skill Sharpeners: Geography • EMC 3746 • © Evan-Moor Corp.

What's Changed?

Demonstrate how human actions can modify the physical environment.

Skill:
Apply geography concepts in context

What You Need

- permission from an adult
- camera
- outdoor space
- various materials, depending on the project
- paper and pencil

What You Do

1. Think about how your actions can change an aspect of the physical environment (outside) at your home. You might consider transforming an outdoor space by changing the landscape. You might create a small pond in your backyard. Discuss your ideas with an adult.

2. Decide what you will do to modify the physical environment. Use the camera to take a "before" picture of the environment you will be changing.

3. Write what you will do and the result you are trying to achieve.

4. Get to work!

5. Once you have finished, take an "after" picture. Show your before and after pictures to your friends and explain what you did.

Environment and Society

Skill:
Write to convey ideas and share opinions

Environment and Society

Water Works

The Earth isn't making more water. We need to make sure the water we have on Earth is being used in the best possible ways. But how do we do that? And how do we address the amount of water that will be needed as the population increases? Write your ideas and opinions to answer these questions.

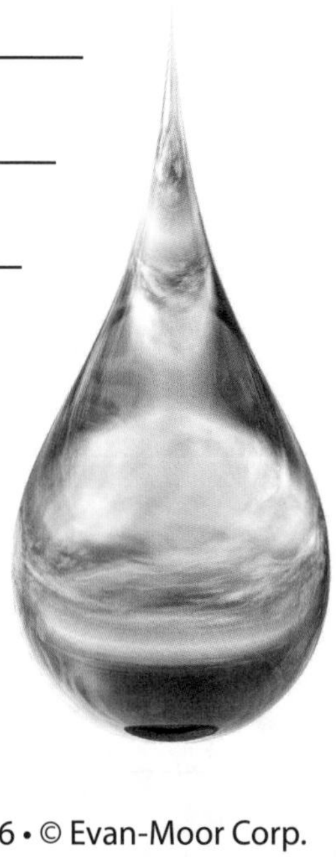

Concept:
People use technology to get what they need from the physical environment.

Goodbye, Cars!

Whenever I travel with my parents, I look out the car window and marvel at all the roads and freeways. I think about what a big job it must have been to build all of them. Initially, it must have involved a lot of physical labor, but as time went on, I imagine machinery such as cranes and bulldozers helped out quite a bit. Now that the roadways are full of cars—practically worldwide—some people are questioning whether that is a good thing. In fact, several major European cities are considering going car-free! People are figuring out how to replace the roads, congestion, honking horns, and pollution with pedestrian zones that consist of walking lanes as well as bike lanes. So which cities are doing this?

Oslo, Norway, has a plan to ban private cars from the city center after 2019. Bike infrastructures, such as pathways, will be put in place. And Oslo will also provide more public transportation options, such as buses and trains.

Several other European cities are joining the car-free movement. Milan, Italy, has a soon-to-be-realized goal of a pedestrian-only zone in the city center. Dublin, Ireland, banned cars from an area of their city center in 2017. Paris, France, has implemented car-free days. They were so well received, the city decided to establish a pedestrian-only zone along the Seine River. Madrid, Spain, has discouraged people from driving cars into the city center and is hoping to soon achieve a pedestrian-first goal. Finally, Brussels, the capital of Belgium, is going to convert a major four-lane road in the city into a pedestrian promenade, or walkway. I guess the next time I visit Europe, I'll be observing city life up close and personal instead of through a car window.

Environment and Society

Fracking

Concept:
People use technology to get what they need from the physical environment.

Define It!

fossil fuels: oil, coal, and gas

fracking: spraying a high-powered mixture at rock to release oil and gas

carbon footprint: the amount of fossil fuels an individual person uses

At some point, Earth will run out of oil, gas, and coal. These are nonrenewable resources—we do not have a way to make more. These resources take billions of years to form inside the earth. However, geologists know that there are more fossil fuels that we have not yet accessed. They are using a method called fracking to help extract oil and gas from the earth. The process of fracking consists of rock being fractured apart by spraying a high-pressure mixture at it. Here's how it works: drilling pipes are placed deep in the ground, then a mixture of water, sand, and chemicals are sprayed at rocks underground. This process fractures the rocks, causing them to release oil or gas, which is then extracted from the ground. The main advantage of fracking is it allows companies to reach areas where natural resources are available that they would not otherwise be able to access. As more gas and oil become available, the price people pay for these resources is reduced.

But there are many serious concerns about fracking. One concern is that fracking requires huge amounts of water to be transported to the site. Both water and transportation are expensive. Also, the chemicals used in the process may enter into the groundwater. Fracking may also cause small earthquakes. In addition, people who are opposed to fracking argue that we need to reduce our carbon footprint by moving away from using fossil fuels and moving toward using alternative, clean energy. Several countries, including France, Germany, and Scotland, have chosen to ban fracking, and several others have halted it until more research is done.

Answer the item.

Based on what you read, what is your opinion about fracking?

_____

_____

_____

Environment and Society

Fracking for shale oil in the Granum area of Alberta, Canada

Fracking for shale oil near a water source in Del Bonita, Alberta, Canada

Environment and Society

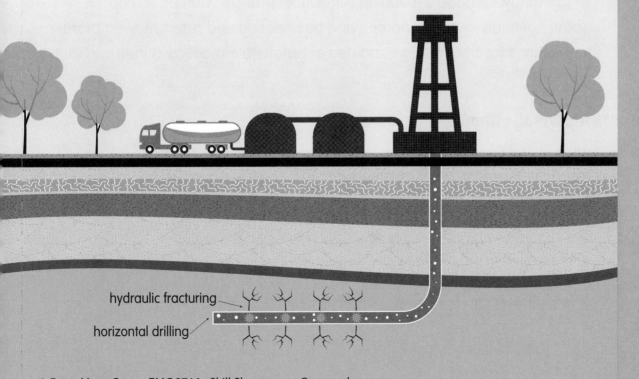

hydraulic fracturing

horizontal drilling

Oh Canada!

Define It!

province: a division of a country similar to a state

resources: materials used by people

hydroelectricity: using moving water to make energy

Canada is a country in North America with ten provinces and three territories. Canada's capital is Ottawa, and its major cities include Toronto, Montreal, Calgary, and Vancouver. Over 36 million people live in Canada, and about 63% of its total energy comes from renewable resources, or resources that can be replenished naturally over time.

Canada's abundant rain and snow provides it with a lot of water—an important natural resource. Currently, hydroelectricity is the major form of usable energy produced from flowing water. To produce hydroelectricity, flowing water is directed at the blades of a turbine, making them spin, which causes an electrical generator connected to the turbine to spin as well, and thus generate electricity.

Moving water is the most important renewable energy source in Canada, providing about 60% of Canada's electricity generation. In fact, Canada is the second largest producer of hydroelectricity in the world.

Canada also uses biomass, or plant matter and animal waste, to generate electricity. It also produces electricity from solar, tidal, and wind energy. Canada's focus on renewable energy sources will no doubt continue to power homes and businesses and result in even more innovations for the creation and use of renewable resources there.

Answer the item.

What natural resource is imperative to Canada's renewable energy resources? Explain why it is important.

_____

_____

_____

A water hydropower
station in Canada

CANADA

Environment and Society

Photovoltaic solar panels
on a solar power farm in
the rural area of Southern
Ontario, Canada

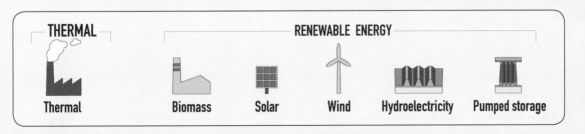

THERMAL	RENEWABLE ENERGY				
Thermal	Biomass	Solar	Wind	Hydroelectricity	Pumped storage

Skill:
Demonstrate
understanding
of geography
concepts

Changing Resources

Read the statement. Write *true* or *false*.

1. Pedestrian zones are for people and bikes. _____

2. Each person's carbon footprint means how much fossil fuels and gases they use. _____

3. Resources are things people use. _____

4. Fracking is a way to get water out of the ground. _____

5. Fossil fuels are coal, oil, and gas. _____

6. A province in Canada is like a state in the United States. _____

7. Biomass cannot be used to generate electricity. _____

8. Hydroelectricity is electricity produced from water. _____

Think About It

Think about how you can reduce your carbon footprint. Write things you and your family can do that are realistic and achievable.

_____

_____

_____

_____

_____

_____

_____

_____

Environment and Society

Skill Sharpeners: Geography • EMC 3746 • © Evan-Moor Corp.

City Planning

Using a map of your town or city, select a potential car-free zone. Then write a letter to the city council proposing your plan.

Skill:
Apply geography concepts in context

What You Need

- Internet access
- map of your area
- highlighter
- pen and paper

What You Do

1. Look at the sample map below.

2. Then print out a map of your town or city.

3. On the map, use a pencil to draw an outline around the area that you think should be a car-free zone. Then highlight the entire area.

4. Next, write a letter to the city council proposing that this area become a car-free zone. Describe the benefits of banning cars in the zone. Include a copy of your map for the council to review.

5. Send your letter to the city council and/or share your plan with others.

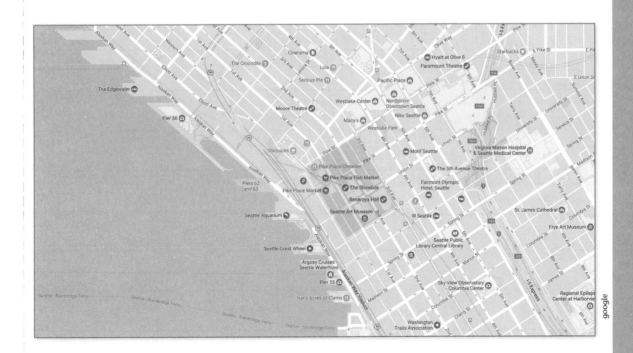

Environment and Society

Skill:

Write narrative text about real-world situations

Environment and Society

Can Car-Free Work for Everyone?

Imagine that the city council implemented your plan for a car-free zone. Is it working well for everyone? How are supplies being brought to the stores and restaurants? Is there public transportation around the perimeter of the area? Can police and firefighters still do their jobs? Write a description of how the car-free zone is working, and try to include the answers to these questions.

_____

_____

_____

_____

_____

_____

_____

_____

_____

_____

_____

_____

Concept:
The human and physical characteristics of places are the settings for events in the past.

The Warship *Vasa*

After visiting the Vasa Maritime Museum, I got into the car and closed my eyes, hoping to take a quick nap. But my imagination was not tired. It took me back in time…

There I was, standing at the edge of the harbor in Stockholm, Sweden, on August 10, 1628…

A large crowd of people had gathered. On orders of the King, a huge warship, the *Vasa*, had been constructed. The ship was set to sail toward Poland and the Baltic Sea to fight a war. Onboard the ship were the crew, 64 cannons, weapons, food, tools, coins, and many other supplies. The vessel drifted out into the harbor.

Suddenly, a gust of wind made the ship lean. Another gust of wind blew the whole ship fully onto its side. Water started pouring into the ship. Everyone onboard climbed to the parts of the vessel that were still above water—including the mast. I couldn't believe this was actually happening! Boats scattered about the harbor, racing to save as many people as they could. But they couldn't save the ship. It sank to the bottom of the harbor.

The *Vasa* remained there for 333 years. In 1961, it was hauled up from the ocean floor, reconstructed, and preserved at a museum.

Concept:
The human and physical characteristics of places are the settings for events in the past.

Sea Pirates

Define It!

Viking: a Scandinavian sea pirate and trader

merchant ship: a ship carrying valuables

bow and stern: the front and back of the boat

Long before the warship *Vasa* was built, Sweden, as well as the Scandinavian countries of Norway and Denmark, were known for Vikings. Vikings were sea pirates and traders, and they were also called seafaring warriors. They invaded coastal lands searching for treasures.

The Viking era began around the 8th century. It was around then that the Vikings' first raid surprised monks, who were chosen as victims because of their valuables and lack of defense. Many raids followed, occurring in Britain, northwest France, Ireland, and Scotland. Vikings also preyed upon merchant ships, which carried goods for trade. Vikings eventually settled in what is known today as parts of Russia, Iceland, Greenland, and Newfoundland, which is an island off the east coast of Canada.

Viking ships were designed to sail rough seas for long distances and to easily maneuver through difficult-to-navigate waters. The ships often had a trademark carved dragon's head or another circular object protruding from the bow and stern.

The Viking era continued until around the 11th century.

Answer the items.

1. Why do you think the Vikings lived as they did?

   _____

   _____

2. Why do you think Vikings used a trademark design on the front of their ships?

   _____

   _____

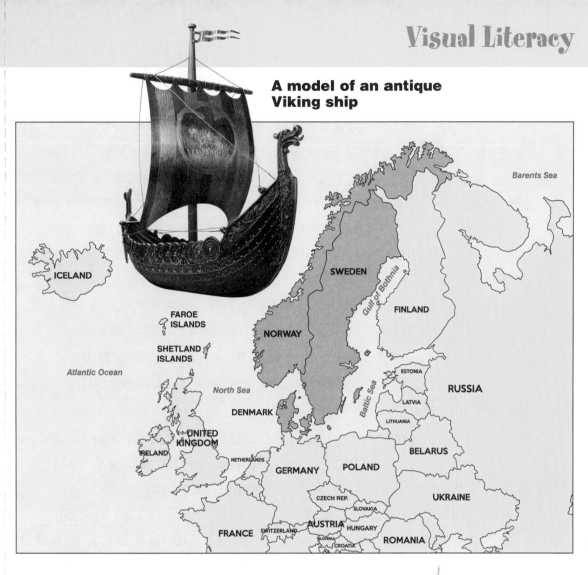

A model of an antique Viking ship

A replica of a Viking longboat

The Uses of Geography

119

Concept:
The human and physical characteristics of places are the settings for events in the past.

Sunken Treasures

Define It!

scuttling: purposely destroying and sinking a ship

artifacts: remains from the past

port: a landing place for ships

There have been many shipwrecks around the world. Some of them were caused because the ships were poorly designed, making them unstable for the load they carried. Some wrecks were caused by ships colliding with icebergs or other ships. In some cases, ships encountered bad weather, high winds, rough seas, or icy conditions. Equipment failure has also caused vessels to sink.

Some ships were destroyed during warfare or by scuttling. Many shipwrecks have recently been discovered, and divers have recovered some of their artifacts.

America's most famous shipwreck is the USS *Arizona*. It was struck during a surprise attack on Pearl Harbor, Hawaii, on December 7, 1941. The *Andrea Doria* was an Italian ocean liner that sank after colliding with a Swedish ship while trying to reach port in New York City in 1956. The *Doña Paz* was a ferry that sunk in 1987 when it ran into an oil tanker while sailing near Manila in the Philippines. The *Titanic* may be the most famous shipwreck in the world. Built in Ireland, it was the largest luxury passenger ship of its time. In 1912, while crossing the Atlantic Ocean, it sank after colliding with an iceberg about 400 miles (644 km) off the coast of Newfoundland.

Answer the items.

1. Do you think some of these shipwrecks could have been avoided? Explain your answer.

_____

_____

2. What method of travel do you think is more dangerous: ship, plane, or car?

_____

Skill Sharpeners: Geography • EMC 3746 • © Evan-Moor Corp.

Sinking of the *Titanic* – The lifeboats row away from the ship on April 15, 1912, as depicted in a British newspaper.

A painting of the *Andrea Doria* colliding with the Swedish ship, *Stockholm*

The USS *Arizona* Memorial in Pearl Harbor – The battleship sunk during a Japanese attack on Pearl Harbor on December 7, 1941. The ship is visible directly beneath the memorial.

The Uses of Geography

Skill:
Demonstrate
understanding
of geography
concepts

Sea Travel

Read the statement. Write *true* or *false*.

1. Vikings are also known as sea pirates. _____

2. The bow and stern are the sides of a boat. _____

3. Merchant ships carry valuable items. _____

4. Scuttling is when ships sink due to bad weather. _____

5. Artifacts are natural items from the ocean. _____

6. A port is a landing place for ships. _____

7. Viking ships were not well-built. _____

8. Weather cannot cause a ship to sink. _____

Think About It

Since ships have sunk throughout history, what items do you think should be onboard all ships to make travel safer for the passengers and crew?

_____

_____

_____

_____

The Uses of Geography

Skill Sharpeners: Geography • EMC 3746 • © Evan-Moor Corp.

Skill:
Apply geography concepts

Craft Stick Boat

Make a boat strong enough to carry cargo without sinking.

What You Need

- 15 to 20 craft sticks
- heavy paper
- tub of water
- scissors

- glue
- colored pencils
- small objects

What You Do

1. Use the craft sticks and glue to build a sturdy boat.

2. Use paper to make a sail.

3. Use colored pencils to decorate the sail.

4. Glue the sail to a craft stick and let it dry.

5. Place the craft stick and sail in a small opening between sticks. Apply glue and hold it there firmly until it is dry.

6. Place small objects as cargo on the boat. Try sailing the boat in a tub of water. See if it floats and can make its journey without tipping. If it does tip over, adjust the cargo and try again.

The Uses of Geography

Skill:
Write informative text to convey information and experiences clearly

Ship Safety

People have been trying to prevent shipwrecks for centuries. What modern technology is available today to reduce or eliminate shipwrecks? Do some research and then write about it.

_____

_____

_____

_____

_____

_____

_____

_____

_____

_____

_____

_____

_____

The Uses of Geography

124

Concept:
Places, regions, and environments change over time.

Weird Things Found in Ice

My parents sometimes go to lectures at the nearby university. One time I went, and the lecture was called "Weird Things Found in Melting Ice."

Here is what I learned. Glaciers are large sheets of ice that slowly move downhill. Some have been around for thousands of years. Many of them are melting rapidly due to climate change. As they melt, people have discovered some weird things in the ice.

In the mountains of Norway, a melting glacier exposed artifacts from thousands of years ago. Several things were discovered, including mittens, shoes, weapons, walking sticks used by Vikings, and arrowheads dated back to the Stone Age, which is a period of time when weapons or tools were made of polished bone, wood, or horn.

In Siberia, Russia, the remains of a woolly mammoth, dated back to 39,000 years ago, were discovered in melting ice. Called Yuka, the creature was so well preserved that its hair was still visible and scientists could even draw blood!

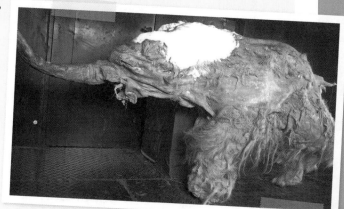

In 1991, in the Otztal region of the Alps between Austria and Italy, a human was discovered sticking out of the ice. The body was originally thought to be a recent tragedy. But scientists dated the person to 5,300 years ago. They named him Otzi because of the region in which he was found.

Finally, on Mount Blanc in France's Alps in 2013, a mountaineer discovered a metal box containing gems from India, including rubies, emeralds, and sapphires! The jewels were likely from a 1966 plane crash. Weird things, indeed!

The Uses of Geography

Concept:
Places, regions, and environments change over time.

Goodbye, Ice

Greenland is the largest island in the world. Nuuk, its capital city, is located at 64° north latitude near the southern tip of the country. The Greenland Ice Sheet covers about 80% of Greenland. It is over 1,500 miles (2,414 km) long—the second-largest sheet of ice on the planet.

Scientists and glaciologists have been observing the ice on Greenland, and their observations are dramatic. Not only is Greenland's huge ice sheet one of the fastest moving areas of ice on the planet, but it is also one of the fastest melting areas. It's losing over 280 billion tons of ice each year. Scientists are also noticing lakes and rivers throughout the ice sheet, and much of the water is draining through moulins, or holes that eventually lead the water to the sea.

According to scientists, if Greenland's ice sheet were to melt completely, the world's oceans would rise by 20 to 23 feet (6 to 7 m). Many coastline areas and cities would probably flood. How quickly will Greenland's ice sheet disappear? That depends on how well we manage and deal with climate change.

Define It!

glaciologist: a person who studies glaciers

moulin: holes in glacial ice that water goes through

climate change: changes in global climate patterns due to levels of atmospheric carbon dioxide produced by the use of fossil fuels

Answer the items.

1. Write two questions about what is happening in Greenland.

   _____

   _____

2. Why do you think one of the largest ice sheets on Earth formed in Greenland?

   _____

   _____

   _____

The Uses of Geography

Skill Sharpeners: Geography • EMC 3746 • © Evan-Moor Corp.

Map of Arctic region

Supraglacial lakes, which are lakes of liquid water on top of a glacier, on the Greenland Ice Sheet

A lake on an ice dome

The Uses of Geography

Where Is the Ice?

Concept:
Places, regions, and environments change over time.

The Uses of Geography

Define It!

polar ice caps: dome-shaped sheets of ice found near the North and South Poles

ice sheet: a mass of glacial land ice extending more than 20,000 square miles (50,000 square km)

ice stream: an area of an ice sheet that moves significantly faster than the surrounding ice

Glaciers, or slowly moving bodies of ice, are found on almost every continent on Earth. Most glaciers are in high mountain areas or polar regions. These regions are dominated by Earth's polar ice caps, the northern resting on the Arctic Ocean and the southern on the continent of Antarctica. About 10% of Earth's land area is covered with glacial ice, including glaciers, ice caps, and the ice sheets of Greenland and Antarctica. Together, these ice sheets contain more than 99% of the freshwater ice on Earth.

Besides Greenland and Antarctica, the most glaciated, or ice-covered, regions of the world include Central Asia, which has the Himalayas, and North America, which has the Cascades, the Rocky Mountains, and very high peaks in Alaska. The Arctic islands are also heavily glaciated.

The largest glacier in the world is the Lambert Glacier in Antarctica. It is over 250 miles (402 km) long and up to 60 miles (100 km) wide. It is one of the ice streams that is draining from the Antarctic Ice Sheet into the sea. Washington State has the largest area of glaciers in the contiguous United States. Its melting glaciers provide 470 billion gallons (1.8 trillion liters) of water each summer.

The world's ice is being monitored as glaciers rapidly melt. Some scientists attribute this as evidence of climate change.

Answer the item.

How do melting glaciers affect Earth?

_____

_____

_____

Greenland's landscape

Ice calving at Margerie Glacier in Glacier Bay National Park, Alaska

Glacier in Antarctica

The Uses of Geography

Skill:
Identify content
vocabulary

It's All About the Ice

Match the definition to its word.

1. holes in ice where water pours through   •   • glacier

2. dome-shaped sheets of ice near the poles   •   • Stone Age

3. a slowly moving body of ice   •   • glaciologist

4. an area of an ice sheet that moves quickly   •
                                                                • moulin

5. a period of time when tools were made of polished bone, wood, or horn   •
                                                                • climate change

6. the term used for human-caused warming of the Earth   •   • ice stream

7. a person who studies glaciers   •   • polar ice caps

Think About It

Many glaciers are in harsh high mountain regions that are hard to get to. How could you study a glacier over a long period of time without being there every day? What methods could you use?

_____

_____

_____

_____

_____

The Uses of Geography

Skill Sharpeners: Geography • EMC 3746 • © Evan-Moor Corp.

A Chunk of Glacial Ice

Skill:
Apply geography concepts

Place artifacts in a tub of water, freeze it, and watch people discover your artifacts in "glacial ice."

What You Need

- plastic tub
- thick towel
- 5 objects that relate to each other
- water
- sand and dirt
- freezer

What You Do

1. Choose five small objects or "artifacts" that relate to each other. Verify that they fit into the plastic tub, then set them aside. Create a fictional story about the artifacts' origins and how they got into the glacier.

2. Fill the tub two-thirds full with water. Mix in some sand and dirt. Place the artifacts in the mixture. Make sure that they cannot be seen on the surface.

3. Place the tub in the freezer and leave it there overnight. Schedule a time for your friends or family to help you with this activity.

4. The next day, take out the tub and set it on a counter an hour or so before your friends or family will be helping you. Allow the ice block to defrost just enough so that you can remove it from the tub.

5. After you remove the block of ice from the tub, set it on a thick towel.

6. Tell your friends or family that you are a glaciologist who found this chunk of ice at the head of a receding glacier. Also mention that the glacier has been known to produce artifacts. As the ice melts, the group will discover the artifacts.

7. Tell the group your fictional story about where the artifacts came from and how they got in the ice.

The Uses of Geography

Skill:
Write to share
observations

Signs of Warmth

Many scientists who are studying climate change agree that Earth is getting warmer due in part to human activity. Many point to melting glaciers as evidence. But what other evidence could there be? Can you think of other data or observations that might indicate a warmer Earth? Write about the other evidence and your observations.

_____

_____

_____

_____

_____

_____

_____

_____

_____

_____

_____

_____

_____

The Uses of Geography

Answer Key

Page 6

Reading

The World in Spatial Terms

Winds on Earth

Define It!

jet stream: winds in Earth's upper atmosphere

atmosphere: the air surrounding Earth

trade winds: the cycle of wind currents moving away from the equator and back

Most tornadoes in the United States move from the southwest to the northeast. One of the reasons for this is that they are driven by the jet stream, or the upper atmosphere wind pattern. Movement of air within Earth's atmosphere is called wind. The main cause of wind is the sun heating the ground unevenly. When this happens, it changes the air pressure, which produces areas of high pressure and low pressure. Wind blows from areas of high pressure to low pressure, which can help produce and drive storms. Wind is also determined by mountains, lakes, canyons, beaches, and other factors.

The sun heats the area around the equator more than at the poles. Warm air at the equator rises and moves toward the poles. As the rising air moves away from the equator, it cools and drops back down to Earth. This cycle is called the trade winds.

The jet stream winds in the upper atmosphere can blow at speeds of about 100 miles per hour (161 kph). The jet stream moves mostly from west to east due to Earth's rotation. But it can fluctuate, or move around. Weather forecasters use the jet stream to determine storm movement. Pilots also use the jet stream—flying with the jet stream can reduce air travel time, but flying against it can take longer.

Answer the items.

1. How does heat cause wind?
   Answers will vary. Ex: When the sun heats the ground unevenly, winds occur.
2. What other professions might use the jet stream to help them?
   Answers will vary. Ex: Sailors or professional bicyclists might use the jet stream.

6 Skill Sharpeners: Geography • EMC 3746 • © Evan-Moor Corp.

Page 8

Reading

The World in Spatial Terms

Hurricanes and Typhoons

Define It!

typhoon: a hurricane-like storm in Southeast Asia or China

sustained: consistently at or above

catastrophic: causing sudden great damage

Hurricanes and typhoons are the largest storms on Earth. They are groups of thunderstorms clustered together in a huge swirling mass of air. In order to be classified as a hurricane or a typhoon, the storm needs to have sustained, or consistent, winds of over 74 miles per hour (119 kph). Hurricanes and typhoons are known for producing massive amounts of rain, flooding, and sometimes even tornadoes as they move over land.

A hurricane and a typhoon are the same thing. It just depends on their location. In the northwestern Pacific Ocean near Southeast Asia and China, the storms are called typhoons. In the Atlantic and northeastern Pacific Ocean, around the Caribbean Sea and off the coast of Mexico, they are called hurricanes. Hurricanes develop over oceans with water temperatures of 80°F (27°C) or higher. Maps are created to show these specific kinds of weather.

Both hurricanes and typhoons are rated for their intensity on the Saffir-Simpson Hurricane Wind Scale. They receive a 1 to 5 rating based on their sustained winds. The strongest of these storms is a Category 5 with wind speeds of over 157 miles per hour (253 kph). Catastrophic, or major, damage will occur from this type of storm. Once the storm hits land, it will gradually weaken and lose its intensity.

Answer the items.

1. Explain the difference between a hurricane and a typhoon.
   Hurricanes develop over oceans with water temperatures of 80°F (27°C) or higher.
2. Have you or someone you know witnessed this type of storm? If so, where and when?
   Answers will vary.

8 Skill Sharpeners: Geography • EMC 3746 • © Evan-Moor Corp.

Page 10

Vocabulary Practice

The World in Spatial Terms

Storms on Earth

Read the statement. Write *true* or *false*.

1. A meteorologist is someone who studies weather. true
2. Hurricanes and typhoons are two very different kinds of storms. false
3. Radar graphics show where rain is falling. true
4. The atmosphere is the water on Earth. false
5. Sustained winds are winds that are consistently at or higher than a certain speed. true
6. The jet stream is the wind or air currents in the upper atmosphere. true
7. Trade winds happen only at the North and South Poles. false
8. Catastrophic damage from a storm means only a few small items were damaged. false

Think About It

What type of storms occur where you live? Hurricanes, typhoons, tornadoes, thunderstorms? What type of storm seems most dangerous to you?

Answers will vary.

10 Skill Sharpeners: Geography • EMC 3746 • © Evan-Moor Corp.

Page 12

Application

The World in Spatial Terms

More Than Just Weather

Meteorologists study weather. But that could mean they need to know quite a few things in addition to weather. What expertise do you think a weathercaster needs to have about maps before he or she presents a weather report on television? Write to explain your thoughts.

Writing will vary.

12 Skill Sharpeners: Geography • EMC 3746 • © Evan-Moor Corp.

Page 14

Reading

The World in Spatial Terms

One Square Inch

Define It!

rainforest: a wet area with dense trees, ferns, and mosses

metropolitan: a large city and surrounding communities

GPS: global positioning system

In a world of city lights and human noise, there are very few quiet places left. But there is at least one—a one-inch spot in Olympic National Park in Washington—possibly the quietest place in the United States. Quiet, in this case, is defined as no human noise at all. So, what do you hear instead? You hear crickets, frogs, birds, mosquitoes, water dripping, the river flowing in the distance, and footsteps of animals nearby in the forest.

The Hoh Rainforest section of the park where the one-inch spot is located is filled with trees, ferns, mosses, and many living things. The area is isolated but only about three hours away from the busy metropolitan area of Seattle. It is a short distance, but it seems like a world away.

So how do you get to this one-inch location? Drive to the Hoh Rainforest and park at the visitor center. Hike 3.2 miles (5.15 km) on the Hoh River Trail. At the 3.2 miles mark, look for a small red-colored stone placed on a moss-covered log. This is the spot. Many people also use global positioning system, or GPS technology, to find the location. Using GPS, the location is 47° 51.959N, 123° 52.221W. Type those numbers into your GPS device, and it will help guide you to the exact location!

Answer the items.

1. How do you think people first located the quietest place in the world?
   Answers will vary.
2. Do you think you can stand 15 minutes of no human noise at all? Explain your answer.
   Answers will vary.

14 Skill Sharpeners: Geography • EMC 3746 • © Evan-Moor Corp.

Page 16

Reading

The World in Spatial Terms

Aurora Borealis

Define It!

aurora borealis: colorful northern lights

light pollution: man-made lights

atmosphere: the air and other elements surrounding Earth

The aurora borealis, also called the northern lights, is an incredible display of moving colors in the upper part of Earth's atmosphere. The bright lights can be pink, green, yellow, orange, blue, violet, and even white. The phenomenon happens all year but is best seen in winter when there is less light pollution, or man-made lights, and crisp, clear cold nights.

Particles from the sun float about in space. Some enter the upper parts of Earth's atmosphere and are drawn toward the magnetic fields around the poles. As the particles pass through our atmosphere, they interact with oxygen, nitrogen, and other elements. The collision of these particles causes the lights. The color the aurora gives off depends on what elements the sun's particles collide with and at what altitude. If the main atmospheric element involved is oxygen, a greenish-yellow or red will be given off. If it is nitrogen, red, violet, and blue colors will be seen. The colors can also mix.

Since the poles are where the sun's particles are drawn, the best places to see the aurora borealis is in far northern latitudes. For example, prime locations include Alaska, northern Canada, Norway, Finland, and Sweden, which are all partially within the Arctic Circle. At times of high amounts of solar activity, the auroras can be seen farther south into England and Scotland, as well as in northern parts of the United States.

Answer the items.

1. Would you like to see the northern lights? If so, which country would you like to view them from? Explain your answer.
   Answers will vary.
2. How do human actions affect the visibility of the northern lights?
   Light pollution from humans makes the lights less visible.

16 Skill Sharpeners: Geography • EMC 3746 • © Evan-Moor Corp.

Page 18

Vocabulary Practice

The World in Spatial Terms

Special Places on Earth

Write the word or words next to its definition.

aurora borealis	light pollution	metropolitan	atmosphere
oxygen	nitrogen	GPS	rainforest

1. an element in the atmosphere that helps to create red, violet, and blue colors nitrogen
2. air and other elements blanketing the Earth atmosphere
3. the lights seen in winter in northern latitudes aurora borealis
4. an element in Earth's atmosphere that helps create greenish-yellow and red colors oxygen
5. a dense area of trees, mosses, and ferns rainforest
6. densely populated city and surrounding communities metropolitan
7. a device used for finding exact locations GPS
8. man-made lights light pollution

Think About It

Which would you want to go and see first: the one-inch spot, the aurora borealis, or the Dark Sky Festival? Tell why.

Answers will vary.

18 Skill Sharpeners: Geography • EMC 3746 • © Evan-Moor Corp.

Page 20

Application

The World in Spatial Terms

Star Gazing

How can cities make sure that natural locations stay free of human light pollution so the night sky can be clearly seen and studied? Write to explain your ideas.

Writing will vary.

20 Skill Sharpeners: Geography • EMC 3746 • © Evan-Moor Corp.

Page 22

Reading

The World in Spatial Terms

Three Cities in Asia

Define It!

finances: business transactions

empire: territories or peoples under the rule of one government

estuary: an area where a river flows into the sea and is filled with fresh and salt water

trade: the action of buying and selling goods and services

Tokyo, Japan, is the most populated metropolitan area in the world. Founded in 1150, about 38 million people live there. Tokyo is also Japan's center of finances, or business and money transactions, as well as government. Nearly the whole population of Tokyo is Japanese, so it is a monoculture. Tokyo is known for having over 6,000 parks and gardens.

Delhi, India, is the second most populated city in the world. About 26 million people live in Delhi. It is one of the world's oldest cities, at almost 5,000 years old. The city is famous for its rickshaws. These three-wheeled, no-doored vehicles are used as taxis all over the city. New Delhi, the capital of India, was built by the British Empire. India gained independence from Great Britain in 1947.

The third most populated city in the world is Shanghai, China. There are about 24 million people living in Shanghai. It was built on an estuary of the Yangtze River. Shanghai is the trade center for China, which means that China sends its products to other countries and receives products from other countries. Shanghai is known for its towering skyscrapers and shopping districts with restaurants.

Answer the items.

1. Do you think there should be a limit on how many people can live within one city? Explain your answer.
   Answers will vary.
2. Which of the three cities above would you want to visit first and why?
   Answers will vary.

22 Skill Sharpeners: Geography • EMC 3746 • © Evan-Moor Corp.

Page 24

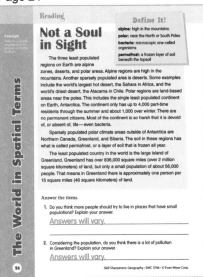

Reading

Not a Soul in Sight

Define It!

alpine: high in the mountains
polar: near the North or South Poles
bacteria: microscopic one-celled organisms
permafrost: a frozen layer of soil beneath the topsoil

The three least populated regions on Earth are alpine zones, deserts, and polar areas. Alpine regions are high in the mountains. Another sparsely populated area is deserts. Some examples include the world's largest hot desert, the Sahara in Africa, and the world's driest desert, the Atacama in Chile. Polar regions are land-based areas near the poles. This includes the single least populated continent on Earth, Antarctica. The continent only has up to 4,000 part-time residents through the summer and about 1,000 over winter. There are no permanent citizens. Most of the continent is so harsh that it is devoid of, or absent of, life—even bacteria.

Sparsely populated polar climate areas outside of Antarctica are Northern Canada, Greenland, and Siberia. The soil in these regions has what is called permafrost, a layer of soil that is frozen all year.

The least populated country in the world is the large island of Greenland. Greenland has over 836,000 square miles (over 2 million square kilometers) of land, but only a small population of about 56,000 people. That means in Greenland there is approximately one person per 15 square miles (40 square kilometers) of land.

Answer the items.

1. Do you think more people should try to live in places that have small populations? Explain your answer.
   Answers will vary.

2. Considering the population, do you think there is a lot of pollution in Greenland? Explain your answer.
   Answers will vary.

The World in Spatial Terms

24

Skill Sharpeners: Geography • EMC 3746 • © Evan-Moor Corp.

Page 26

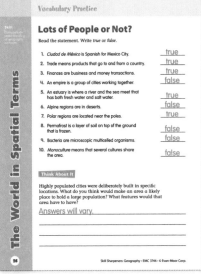

Vocabulary Practice

Lots of People or Not?

Read the statement. Write *true* or *false*.

1. Ciudad de México is Spanish for Mexico City. — true
2. Trade means products that go to from a country. — true
3. Finances are business and money transactions. — true
4. An empire is a group of cities working together. — false
5. An estuary is where a river and the sea meet that has both fresh water and salt water. — true
6. Alpine regions are in deserts. — false
7. Polar regions are located near the poles. — true
8. Permafrost is a layer of soil on top of the ground that is frozen. — false
9. Bacteria are microscopic multicelled organisms. — false
10. Monoculture means that several cultures share the area. — false

Think About It

Highly populated cities were deliberately built in specific locations. What do you think would make an area a likely place to hold a large population? What features would that area have to have?

Answers will vary.

The World in Spatial Terms

26

Skill Sharpeners: Geography • EMC 3746 • © Evan-Moor Corp.

Page 28

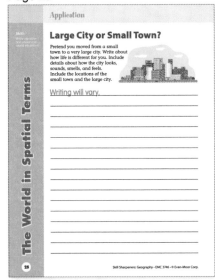

Application

Large City or Small Town?

Pretend you moved from a small town to a very large city. Write about how life is different for you. Include details about how the city looks, sounds, smells, and feels. Include the locations of the small town and the large city.

Writing will vary.

The World in Spatial Terms

28

Skill Sharpeners: Geography • EMC 3746 • © Evan-Moor Corp.

Page 30

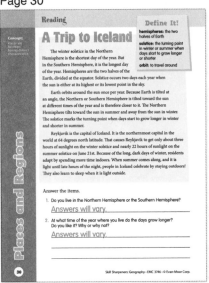

Reading

A Trip to Iceland

Define It!

hemispheres: the two halves of Earth
solstice: the turning point in winter or summer when days start to grow longer or shorter
orbit: to travel around

The winter solstice in the Northern Hemisphere is the shortest day of the year. But in the Southern Hemisphere, it is the longest day of the year. Hemispheres are the two halves of the Earth, divided at the equator. Solstice occurs two days each year when the sun is either at its highest or its lowest point in the sky.

Earth orbits around the sun once per year. Because Earth is tilted at an angle, the Northern or Southern Hemisphere is tilted toward the sun at different times of the year and is therefore closer to it. The Northern Hemisphere tilts toward the sun in summer and away from the sun in winter. The solstice marks the turning point when days start to grow longer in winter and shorter in summer.

Reykjavik is the capital of Iceland. It is the northernmost capital in the world at 64 degrees north latitude. That causes Reykjavik to get only about three hours of sunlight on the winter solstice and 22 hours of sunlight on the summer solstice on June 21st. Because of the long, dark days of winter, residents adapt by spending more time indoors. When summer comes along, and it is light until late hours of the night, people in Iceland celebrate by staying outdoors! They also learn to sleep when it is light outside.

Answer the items.

1. Do you live in the Northern Hemisphere or the Southern Hemisphere?
   Answers will vary.

2. At what time of the year where you live do the days grow longer? Do you like it? Why or why not?
   Answers will vary.

Places and Regions

30

Skill Sharpeners: Geography • EMC 3746 • © Evan-Moor Corp.

Page 32

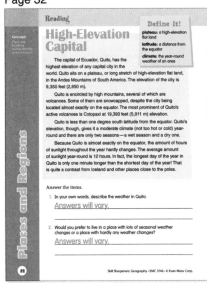

Reading

High-Elevation Capital

Define It!

plateau: a high-elevation flat land
latitude: a distance from the equator
climate: the year-round weather of an area

The capital of Ecuador, Quito, has the highest elevation of any capital city in the world. Quito sits on a plateau, or long stretch of high-elevation flat land, in the Andes Mountains of South America. The elevation of the city is 9,350 feet (2,850 m).

Quito is encircled by high mountains, several of which are volcanoes. Some of them are snowcapped, despite the city being located almost exactly on the equator. The most prominent of Quito's active volcanoes is Cotopaxi at 19,393 feet (5,911 m) elevation.

Quito is less than one degree south latitude from the equator. Quito's elevation, though, gives it a moderate climate (not too hot or cold) year-round and there are only two seasons—a wet season and a dry one.

Because Quito is almost exactly on the equator, the amount of hours of sunlight throughout the year hardly changes. The average amount of sunlight year-round is 12 hours. In fact, the longest day of the year in Quito is only one minute longer than the shortest day of the year! That is quite a contrast from Iceland and other places close to the poles.

Answer the items.

1. In your own words, describe the weather in Quito.
   Answers will vary.

2. Would you prefer to live in a place with lots of seasonal weather changes or a place with hardly any weather changes?
   Answers will vary.

Places and Regions

32

Skill Sharpeners: Geography • EMC 3746 • © Evan-Moor Corp.

Page 34

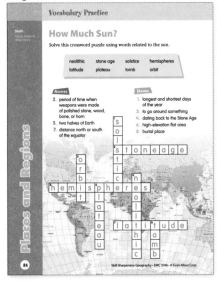

Vocabulary Practice

How Much Sun?

Solve this crossword puzzle using words related to the sun.

neolithic   stone age   solstice   hemispheres
latitude   plateau   tomb   orbit

Across

2. period of time when weapons were made of polished stone, wood, bone, or horn
5. two halves of Earth
7. distance north or south of the equator

Down

1. longest and shortest days
3. to go around something
4. dating back to the Stone Age
6. high-elevation flat area
8. burial place

(crossword answers: solstice, stoneage, orbit, hemispheres, neolithic, plateau, latitude, tomb)

Places and Regions

34

Skill Sharpeners: Geography • EMC 3746 • © Evan-Moor Corp.

Page 36

Application

A Letter Home

Using what you know about daylight hours around the globe, choose a place to live. Then write a letter home describing where you are, what the weather is like, and how you spend your time.

Writing will vary.

Places and Regions

36

Skill Sharpeners: Geography • EMC 3746 • © Evan-Moor Corp.

Page 38

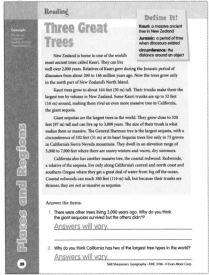

Reading

Three Great Trees

Define It!

Kauri: a massive ancient tree in New Zealand
Jurassic: a period of time when dinosaurs existed
circumference: the distance around an object

New Zealand is home to one of the world's most ancient trees called Kauri. They can live well over 2,000 years. Relatives of Kauri grew during the Jurassic period of dinosaurs from about 200 to 146 million years ago. Now the trees grow only in the north part of New Zealand's North Island.

Kauri trees grow to about 164 feet (50 m) tall. Their trunks make them the largest tree by volume in New Zealand. Some Kauri trunks are up to 52 feet (16 m) around, making them even more massive tree in California, the giant sequoia.

Giant sequoias are the largest trees in the world. They grow close to 320 feet (97 m) tall and can live up to 3,000 years. The size of their trunk is what makes them so massive. The General Sherman tree is the largest sequoia, with a circumference of 102 feet (31 m) at its base! Sequoia trees live only in 75 groves in California's Sierra Nevada mountains. They dwell in an elevation range of 5,000 to 7,000 feet where there are snowy winters and warm, dry summers.

California also has another massive tree, the coastal redwood. Redwoods, a relative of the sequoia, live only along California's central and north coast and southern Oregon where they get a great deal of water from fog off the ocean. Coastal redwoods can reach 380 feet (116 m) tall, but because their trunks are thinner, they are not as massive as sequoias.

Answer the items.

1. There were other trees living 3,000 years ago. Why do you think the giant sequoias survived but the others didn't?
   Answers will vary.

2. Why do you think California has two of the largest tree types in the world?
   Answers will vary.

Places and Regions

38

Skill Sharpeners: Geography • EMC 3746 • © Evan-Moor Corp.

Page 40

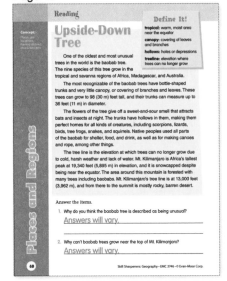

Reading

Upside-Down Tree

Define It!

tropical: warm, moist area near the equator
canopy: covering of leaves and branches
hollows: holes or depressions
treeline: elevation where trees can no longer grow

One of the oldest and most unusual trees in the world is the baobab tree. The nine species of this tree grow in the tropical and savanna regions of Africa, Madagascar, and Australia.

The most recognizable of the baobab trees have bottle-shaped trunks and very little canopy, or covering of branches and leaves. These trees can grow to 98 (30 m) feet tall, and their trunks can measure up to 36 feet (11 m) in diameter.

The flowers of the tree give off a sweet-and-sour smell that attracts bats and insects at night. The trunks have hollows in them, making them perfect homes for all kinds of creatures, including scorpions, lizards, birds, tree frogs, snakes, and squirrels. Native peoples used all parts of the baobab for shelter, food, and drink, as well as for making canoes and rope, among other things.

The tree line is the elevation at which trees can no longer grow due to cold, harsh weather and lack of water. Mt. Kilimanjaro is Africa's tallest peak at 19,340 feet (5,895 m) in elevation, and it is snowcapped despite being near the equator. The area around this mountain is forested with many trees including baobabs. Mt. Kilimanjaro's tree line is at 13,000 feet (3,962 m), and from there to the summit is mostly rocky, barren desert.

Answer the items.

1. Why do you think the baobab tree is described as being unusual?
   Answers will vary.

2. Why can't boobab trees grow near the top of Mt. Kilimanjaro?
   Answers will vary.

Places and Regions

40

Skill Sharpeners: Geography • EMC 3746 • © Evan-Moor Corp.

Skill Sharpeners: Geography • EMC 3746 • © Evan-Moor Corp.

Page 42

Vocabulary Practice

Where Are the Trees?

Find these words about trees in the word search.
Hint: Some are backwards.

baobab	kilimanjaro	tree line	methuselah
jurassic	sequoia	redwood	
extremophile	bristlecone	kauri	

Places and Regions

Page 44

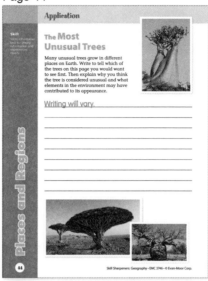

Application

The Most Unusual Trees

Many unusual trees grow in different places on Earth. Write to tell which of the trees on this page you would ever to see first. Then explain why you think the tree is considered unusual and what elements in the environment may have contributed to its appearance.

Writing will vary.

Places and Regions

Page 46

Reading

A United Germany

Define It!
Cold War: a period of time when there was a fear of war between countries
diplomat: someone who represents a country
Tor auf: means "Open the gate" in German

When World War II ended, Germany was split into four territories in 1945. The eastern part went to the Soviet Union and the western parts went to the United States, Great Britain, and France.

Because of this new division, the city of Berlin, Germany, became West Berlin and East Berlin. Over time, tensions flared up between the two sides. On August 13, 1961, the Soviet Union started to erect a 12-foot (3.7-m) wall of concrete to separate the sides. This caused thousands of people to quickly leave East Berlin.

Hostility continued to grow between the Soviet Union and the West. This led to a period of history called the Cold War, during which people feared a real war could break out between the two countries.

After the wall was finished, 12 checkpoint stations were set up. The most well-known of them was called Checkpoint Charlie, located in the center of Berlin. Only diplomats or other officials with proper papers could cross the border at a checkpoint.

Eventually, the Cold War ended, and on November 9, 1989, the Soviet Union said "Tor auf," meaning "Open the gate!" Over two million people crossed the border that weekend alone! In the end, on October 3, 1990, East Germany and West Germany were officially reunited.

Answer the item.

Why do you think so many people crossed between East and West Germany after the wall was taken down?

Answers will vary.

Places and Regions

Page 48

Reading

Sharing a Continent

Define It!
blizzard: a severe snowstorm
claim: stating the land is owned by a country
treaty: a formal agreement among nations
resources: materials from Earth used by people

Antarctica is the coldest, windiest, and driest continent on Earth. The entire landmass also holds 90% of the world's ice in the form of glaciers. But actually, little moisture falls. Antarctica gets less precipitation than most of the Sahara, the world's largest hot desert. When it does snow in Antarctica, the snow blows like a desert dust storm in whiteout blizzards.

In the past, several countries had made claims to the continent, including Great Britain, France, and Argentina. But none of the claims were recognized by any country because of the Antarctic Treaty of 1959.

This treaty was signed by the 12 countries who had been active exploring in and around Antarctica. Since 1959, 41 more countries have signed the treaty. Specific provisions of the agreement include:
1. Use the land for peaceful purposes only.
2. All countries cooperate toward scientific exploration.
3. The science is to be shared by the international community.

Some experts believe the discovery of valuable natural resources in Antarctica could lead countries to want to claim land there again, but so far the treaty is still being followed.

Answer the Items.

1. Why do you think 41 more countries have signed the Antarctic Treaty?
Answers will vary. Ex: The other countries probably want to explore Antarctica, too.

2. Do you think Antarctica should remain under the rules of the treaty?
Answers will vary.

Places and Regions

Page 50

Vocabulary Practice

Managing Lands

Write the word next to its definition.

| Tor auf | diplomat | supercontinent | continent |
| Cold War | claim | treaty | resources |

1. when there was hostility between nations and a threat of war — Cold War
2. an agreement between nations on how to use or share land — treaty
3. someone who works for a country — diplomat
4. one of seven large landmasses on Earth — continent
5. natural materials taken from Earth — resources
6. means "Open the gate" in German — Tor auf
7. ancient continent of landmasses clumped together — supercontinent
8. when a country says it owns land — claim

Think About It

What characteristics might a large tract of land have that would make countries want to claim it?
Answers will vary.

Places and Regions

Page 52

Application

Changing Spaces

People change how they use different spaces all the time. For example, has your room always belonged to you, or was it your big brother's or sister's before it was yours? Has your family remodeled your house and changed the garage into a living room? Did your school build new classrooms or a new cafeteria or gymnasium? Write about a space that you know of that has changed.

Writing will vary.

Places and Regions

Page 54

Reading

Colliding Plates

Define It!
introduced species: animals brought to an area by people
endemic: found nowhere else
tectonic plates: parts of the Earth's crust that move continuously

The Galápagos Islands are about 600 miles (966 km) off the coast of Ecuador. They consist of 13 major islands and many smaller ones. The Galápagos Islands are famous for their unusual wildlife. The animals that live there are classified into three categories. The first is native creatures that are natural to the islands but also live elsewhere. One example is the peregrine falcon. The second is introduced species, such as goats, that were brought to the islands by humans. The third and most prolific example of wildlife on the Galápagos Islands is its endemic species. These are creatures that live nowhere else in the world. The Galápagos giant tortoise is a well-known example of an endemic species. It is the largest living species of tortoise.

The Galápagos Islands were formed by the collision of tectonic plates. Tectonic plates are parts of the Earth's crust that are in constant motion. The Nazca Plate and the South American Plate meet at the Galápagos Islands and collide beneath the Pacific Ocean, which causes volcanic activity. Volcanoes created the islands and continue to do so today. There have been over 50 eruptions there in the last 200 years.

Answer the items.

1. What kinds of relationships do you think the endemic species and the introduced species have?
Answers will vary.

2. Have you ever seen a volcano or evidence of volcanic activity? If so, where?
Answers will vary.

Physical Systems

Page 56

Reading

Landforms on Earth

Define It!
landform: a physical feature of the land
erosion: gradual wearing away of land by natural forces
archipelago: a group of islands clustered together
peninsula: land surrounded by water on three sides

About two-thirds of Earth is covered by water. About one-fourth of Earth is covered by land. The small amount left, about 10%, is covered in ice.

The land on Earth is in different shapes called landforms. These take on various shapes depending on how they were formed and how they have eroded due to wind, rain, frost, ice, or chemicals. Plate tectonics, or the collision of Earth's plates, also shapes the land.

Some of the major landforms on Earth include mountains, volcanoes, and mountain ranges. There are hills, which are more rounded and lower than mountains. There are valleys, which are formed between mountains and hills. Valleys often have rivers and tributaries, or smaller streams, running through them. There are plateaus, or high-elevation flat areas, and mesas, which are plateaus with steep sides. There are plains, which are large areas of flat land. Plains often have fertile soil good for growing crops. Islands are areas of land completely surrounded by water. They can be tiny or as large as a continent such as Australia. Groups of islands clustered together are called archipelagos. There are deserts with sparse vegetation. And there are peninsulas, or areas of land surrounded by water on three sides, such as Florida.

Answer the items.

1. Of all of Earth's landforms, which one describes the area where you live?
Answers will vary.

2. What type of landform would you like to know more about? Explain your answer.
Answers will vary.

Physical Systems

Page 58

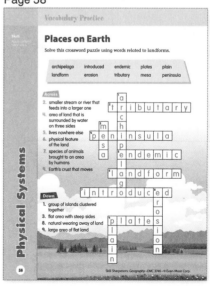

Vocabulary Practice

Places on Earth

Solve this crossword puzzle using words related to landforms.

| archipelago | introduced | endemic | plates | plain |
| landform | erosion | tributary | mesa | peninsula |

Across
2. smaller stream or river that feeds into a larger one — tributary
4. area of land that is surrounded by water on three sides — peninsula
5. lives nowhere else — endemic
6. physical feature of the land — landform
7. species of animals brought to an area by humans — introduced
8. Earth's crust that moves — plates

Down
1. group of islands clustered together
2. flat area with steep sides
8. natural wearing away of land — erosion
9. large area of flat land — plain

Physical Systems

Application

New Landforms

Pretend a new landform appeared near where you live. What physical process caused it to be created? How did it change Earth's surface? Write a realistic fiction account of this event.

Writing will vary.

Physical Systems

Reading

Las Vegas, The Meadows

Define It!

oasis: a fertile green area in the desert

reservoir: a man-made lake

aquifer: an underground source of water

landscaping: altering the vegetation of land to use less water

The sprawling city of Las Vegas is about 120 miles (193 km) away from Death Valley. *Las Vegas* means "The Meadows" in Spanish. Before there was a city, the area had spring water that fed grasses that gave the city its name. It was an oasis in the desert— a fertile spot where water is found. Today, there are over two million people living in Las Vegas and tens of millions of tourists vacationing there each year.

Las Vegas is right in the middle of the Mojave Desert. It gets very little precipitation, yet the city keeps on growing. So how does it get water?

Hoover Dam was finished in 1936. It took 5 years for Lake Mead, the man-made lake, or reservoir, behind it to fill. Now, Lake Mead supplies 90% of Las Vegas's water, as well as some to Arizona and parts of California. But the lake is drying up and could be gone in the next five or so years. So what else can Las Vegas do for water? Up to 93% of the water in Las Vegas is treated and reused—hotels use recycled water in showers and sinks. Many people have received money from the city for converting their lawns to water-free landscaping. The city is also looking into using water from aquifers. But those aquifers provide springs and habitats for plants and animals, so this plan is controversial. For the time being, Las Vegas's water situation remains unresolved.

Answer the items.

1. Do you think Las Vegas should stop building more hotels and houses while they figure out a reliable water source? Explain your answer.

   Answers will vary.

2. Is using an aquifer as a source of water a good idea? Why or why not?

   Answers will vary.

Physical Systems

Reading

Oasis in the Desert

Define It!

oasis: a place of plants and water in the middle of the desert

agua caliente: means "hot water" in Spanish

archaeological: related to studies of past civilizations

Just outside the Las Vegas city boundary is Red Rock Canyon Conservation Area. Red Rock Canyon is an area of towering red rock canyon walls. There are springs, waterfalls, and small pools of water— a little oasis in the desert. This area is home to wildlife such as the desert tortoise, bighorn sheep, and wild burro.

Agua Caliente Park is just outside Tucson, Arizona. *Agua caliente* means "hot water" in Spanish. There is archaeological evidence that shows people have been coming there for at least 5,000 years. The park has warm spring-fed waters, palm trees, and hiking trails.

In Israel, Ein Gedi is along the coast of the Dead Sea. People have been visiting this oasis for nearly 3,000 years. Today, the area is a nature reserve for the plants and animals that rely on the spring-fed waters.

Some say the world's most beautiful oasis is Chebika in Tunisia in northern Africa. It is called the Qasr el-Shams, which is Arabic for "castle of the sun." Several scenes from *Star Wars IV* were filmed there.

Answer the items.

1. Why do you think people, plants, and animals are drawn to an oasis?

   Answers will vary.

2. Which of these oases would you like to go to first? Explain your answer.

   Answers will vary.

Physical Systems

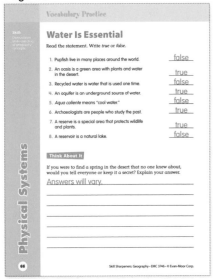

Vocabulary Practice

Water Is Essential

Read the statement. Write *true* or *false*.

1. Pupfish live in many places around the world. — false

2. An oasis is a green area with plants and water in the desert. — true

3. Recycled water is water that is used one time. — false

4. An aquifer is an underground source of water. — true

5. *Agua caliente* means "cool water." — false

6. Archaeologists are people who study the past. — true

7. A reserve is a special area that protects wildlife and plants. — true

8. A reservoir is a natural lake. — false

Think About It

If you were to find a spring in the desert that no one knew about, would you tell everyone or keep it a secret? Explain your answer.

Answers will vary.

Physical Systems

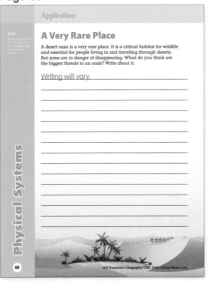

Application

A Very Rare Place

A desert oasis is a very rare place. It is a critical habitat for wildlife and essential for people living in and traveling through deserts. But some are in danger of disappearing. What do you think are the biggest threats to an oasis? Write about it.

Writing will vary.

Physical Systems

Reading

Breathing at the Top of the World

Define It!

hypoxia: a condition of altitude sickness

highlander: a person who is able to live at high elevations

adaptation: adjusting to certain conditions

Only a few groups of people have adapted to living at high elevations for extended periods of time. High elevations are considered areas over 13,000 feet (4,000 m).

High elevations have less oxygen in the air. People who climb to high altitudes may have symptoms of altitude sickness, or reduced oxygen, including headaches, vomiting, difficulty sleeping, impaired thinking, and the inability to keep active. These conditions are known as hypoxia. The best remedy is to go back downhill. At extreme elevations, a person can die from hypoxia.

Three groups of people called highlanders are known for being able to live at high elevations. The first are the people who live in the Andes Mountains of South America. They have adapted to the altitude because their bodies can carry more oxygen in each red blood cell than a normal person.

The next are the people of the Tibetan Plateau in the Himalayas in Asia. Their adaptation is that they breathe more often. The last are the Ethiopian highlanders in East Africa. They have also adapted, but the explanation for how they have adapted is still a mystery. One fact known about all three groups is that each generation who lives at a high altitude becomes better adapted to it.

Answer the items.

1. Why do you think each generation of people living at high altitudes becomes better adapted to it?

   Answers will vary.

2. What is the highest elevation you have been at? Did you feel the effects of being at a higher elevation?

   Answers will vary.

Human Systems

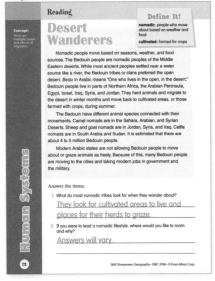

Reading

Desert Wanderers

Define It!

nomadic: people who move about based on weather and food

cultivated: farmed for crops

Nomadic people move based on seasons, weather, and food sources. The Bedouin people are nomadic peoples of the Middle Eastern deserts. While most ancient peoples settled near a water source like a river, the Bedouin tribes or clans preferred the open desert. *Bedu* in Arabic means "One who lives in the open, in the desert." Bedouin people live in parts of Northern Africa, the Arabian Peninsula, Egypt, Israel, Iraq, Syria, and Jordan. They herd animals and migrate to the desert in winter months and move back to cultivated areas, or those farmed with crops, during summer.

The Bedouin have different animal species connected with their movements. Camel nomads are in the Sahara, Arabian, and Syrian Deserts. Sheep and goat nomads are in Jordan, Syria, and Iraq. Cattle nomads are in South Arabia and Sudan. It is estimated that there are about 4 to 5 million Bedouin people.

Modern Arabic states are not allowing Bedouin people to move about or graze animals as freely. Because of this, many Bedouin people are moving to the cities and taking modern jobs in government and the military.

Answer the items.

1. What do most nomadic tribes look for when they wander about?

   They look for cultivated areas to live and places for their herds to graze.

2. If you were to lead a nomadic lifestyle, where would you like to roam and why?

   Answers will vary.

Human Systems

Vocabulary Practice

Nomadic People

Match the definition to its word.

1. name for a person who lives at high elevations — highlander

2. term for a group of people who move from place to place — nomadic

3. medical issue for those suffering from lack of oxygen — hypoxia

4. area that is farmed for crops — cultivated

5. name of a guide famous for being able to withstand high elevations — Sherpa

6. when people have acquired traits that help them survive — adaptation

Think About It

If you lived with a nomadic group of people, what modern items would you miss the most? Or, could a nomadic group have all the amenities of a modern society?

Answers will vary.

Human Systems

Application

Choose Your Life

Which nomadic lifestyle do you think is attainable for you: trekking and living at high elevations or in the desert? What would be easy parts of that life for you to adjust to? What would be more difficult? Realistically, do you think you could adapt to a nomadic lifestyle? Choose the life you think would be best for you and write about it.

Writing will vary.

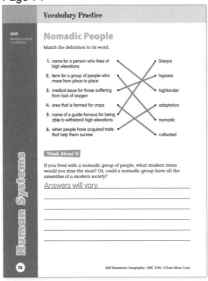

Human Systems

Skill Sharpeners: Geography • EMC 3746 • © Evan-Moor Corp.

Page 78

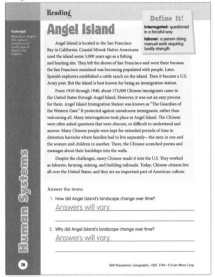

Angel Island

Define It!
interrogated: questioned in a forceful way
laborer: a person doing manual work requiring bodily strength

Concept: Migration shapes the cultural and physical landscape of places and regions.

Angel Island is located in the San Francisco Bay in California. Coastal Miwok Native Americans used the island some 3,000 years ago as a fishing and hunting site. They left the shores of San Francisco mainland because the San Francisco mainland was becoming populated with people. Later, Spanish explorers established a cattle ranch on the island. Then it became a U.S. Army post. But the island is best known for being an immigration station.

From 1910 through 1940, about 175,000 Chinese immigrants came to the United States through Angel Island. However, it was not an easy process for them. Angel Island Immigration Station was known as "The Guardian of the Western Gate." It protected against unwelcome immigrants, rather than welcoming all. Many interrogations took place at Angel Island. The Chinese were often asked questions that were obscure, or difficult to understand and answer. Many Chinese people were kept for extended periods of time in detention barracks where families had to live separately—the men in one and the women and children in another. There, the Chinese scratched poems and messages about their hardships into the walls.

Despite the challenges, many Chinese made it into the U.S. They worked as laborers, farming, mining, and building railroads. Today, Chinese citizens live all over the United States, and they are an important part of American culture.

Answer the items.

1. How did Angel Island's landscape change over time?
   Answers will vary.

2. Why did Angel Island's landscape change over time?
   Answers will vary.

Page 80

Shelter in Europe

Define It!
immigrant: a person who comes to live permanently in a foreign country
refugee: a person fleeing a war or conflict
migrant: a person who moves from place to place to find work or safety and shelter
detention center: a building that houses immigrants

Concept: Migration shapes the cultural and physical landscape of places and regions.

People from Africa, the Middle East, and southern Asia are pouring into Europe. They mainly come through Greece and Italy, as these countries are closer to the Mediterranean Basin where the immigrants are from. Some of the immigrants are crossing the borders illegally, and border patrols in Europe are tightening their security.

Refugees, such as people from Syria and Afghanistan, are fleeing war. Those from Eritrea, a small country in Africa, are escaping forced labor.

Many of these immigrants are housed in camps, and some are placed in detention centers. Most of these facilities are overcrowded and do not have enough resources to provide the immigrants with basic necessities.

As immigrants and migrants enter European countries, some people worry that there are not enough jobs available to support them. Some people don't want the immigrants to live there. Conversely, some people are working hard to help them start a new life.

Immigration and migration are ongoing challenging issues for many countries.

Answer the item.

Do you think all people fleeing wars and poverty should be allowed to go to new countries and start a new life?
Answers will vary.

Page 82

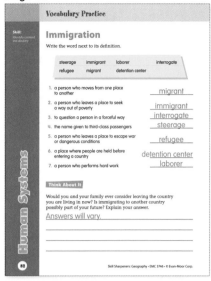

Immigration

Skill: Identify content vocabulary

Write the word next to its definition.

steerage	immigrant	laborer	interrogate
refugee	migrant	detention center	

1. a person who moves from one place to another — migrant
2. a person who leaves a place to seek a way out of poverty — immigrant
3. to question a person in a forceful way — interrogate
4. the name given to third-class passengers — steerage
5. a person who leaves a place to escape war or dangerous conditions — refugee
6. a place where people are held before entering a country — detention center
7. a person who performs hard work — laborer

Think About It

Would you and your family ever consider leaving the country you are living in now? Is immigrating to another country possibly part of your future? Explain your answer.
Answers will vary.

Page 84

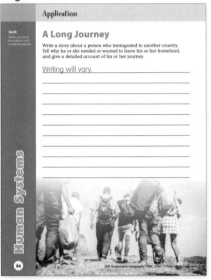

A Long Journey

Skill: Write narrative text about real-world situations

Write a story about a person who immigrated to another country. Tell why he or she needed or wanted to leave his or her homeland, and give a detailed account of his or her journey.

Writing will vary.

Page 86

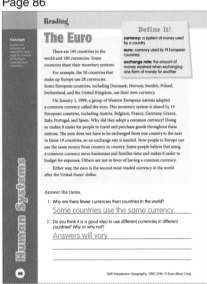

The Euro

Define It!
currency: a system of money used by a country
euro: currency used by 19 European countries
exchange rate: the amount of money received when exchanging one form of money for another

Concept: Economic systems of countries and regions consist of multiple coordinated activities.

There are 195 countries in the world and 180 currencies. Some countries share their monetary systems.

For example, the 50 countries that make up Europe use 28 currencies. Some European countries, including Denmark, Norway, Sweden, Poland, Switzerland, and the United Kingdom, use their own currency.

On January 1, 1999, a group of Western European nations adopted a common currency called the euro. This monetary system is shared by 19 European countries, including Austria, Belgium, France, Germany, Greece, Italy, Portugal, and Spain. Why did they adopt a common currency? Doing so makes it easier for people to travel and purchase goods throughout these nations. The euro does not have to be exchanged from one country to the next in those 19 countries, so no exchange rate is needed. Now people in Europe can use the same money from country to country. Some people believe that using a common currency saves businesses and families time and makes it easier to budget for expenses. Others are not in favor of having a common currency.

Either way, the euro is the second most-traded currency in the world after the United States' dollar.

Answer the items.

1. Why are there fewer currencies than countries in the world?
   Some countries use the same currency.

2. Do you think it is a good idea to use different currencies in different countries? Why or why not?
   Answers will vary.

Page 88

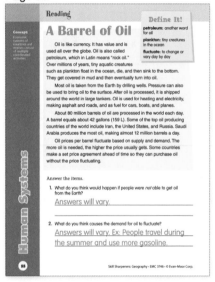

A Barrel of Oil

Define It!
petroleum: another word for oil
plankton: tiny creatures in the ocean
fluctuate: to change or vary day by day

Concept: Economic systems of countries and regions consist of multiple coordinated activities.

Oil is like currency. It has value and is used all over the globe. Oil is also called petroleum, which in Latin means "rock oil." Over millions of years, tiny aquatic creatures such as plankton float in the ocean, die, and then sink to the bottom. They get covered in mud and then eventually turn into oil.

Most oil is taken from the Earth by drilling wells. Pressure can also be used to bring oil to the surface. After oil is processed, it is shipped around the world in large tankers. Oil is used for heating and electricity, making asphalt and roads, and as fuel for cars, boats, and planes.

About 80 million barrels of oil are processed in the world each day. A barrel equals about 42 gallons (159 L). Some of the top oil producing countries of the world include Iran, the United States, and Russia. Saudi Arabia produces the most oil, making almost 12 million barrels a day.

Oil prices per barrel fluctuate based on supply and demand. The more oil is needed, the higher the price usually gets. Some countries make a set price agreement ahead of time so they can purchase oil without the price fluctuating.

Answer the items.

1. What do you think would happen if people were *not* able to get oil from the Earth?
   Answers will vary.

2. What do you think causes the demand for oil to fluctuate?
   Answers will vary. Ex: People travel during the summer and use more gasoline.

Page 90

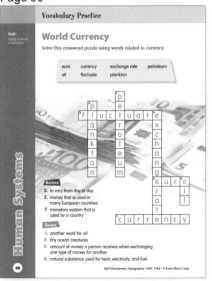

World Currency

Skill: Apply content vocabulary

Solve this crossword puzzle using words related to currency.

euro	currency	exchange rate	petroleum
oil	fluctuate	plankton	

Across
3. to vary from day to day
5. money that is used in many European countries
7. monetary system that is used by a country

Down
1. another word for *oil*
2. tiny ocean creatures
4. amount of money a person receives when exchanging one type of money for another
6. natural substance used for heat, electricity, and fuel

(Crossword answers: fluctuate, plankton, petroleum, exchange rate, euro, oil, currency)

Page 92

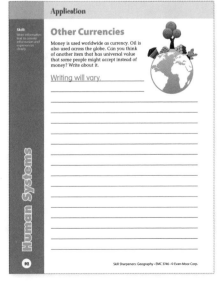

Other Currencies

Skill: Write informative text to convey information and experiences clearly

Money is used worldwide as currency. Oil is also used across the globe. Can you think of another item that has universal value that some people might accept instead of money? Write about it.

Writing will vary.

Page 94

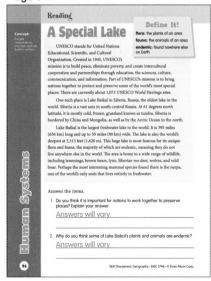

A Special Lake

Define It!
flora: the plants of an area
fauna: the animals of an area
endemic: found nowhere else on Earth

Concept: People cooperate to manage and use Earth's surface.

UNESCO stands for United Nations Educational, Scientific, and Cultural Organization. Created in 1945, UNESCO's mission is to build peace, eliminate poverty, and create intercultural cooperation and partnerships through education, the sciences, culture, communication, and information. Part of UNESCO's mission is to bring nations together to protect and preserve some of the world's most special places. There are currently about 1,073 UNESCO World Heritage sites.

One such place is Lake Baikal in Siberia, Russia, the oldest lake in the world. Siberia is a vast area in south-central Russia. At 61 degrees north latitude, it is mostly cold, frozen, grassland known as tundra. Siberia is bordered by China and Mongolia, as well as by the Arctic Ocean to the north.

Lake Baikal is the largest freshwater lake in the world. It is 395 miles (636 km) long and up to 50 miles (80 km) wide. The lake is also the world's deepest at 5,315 feet (1,620 m). This huge lake is most famous for its unique flora and fauna, the majority of which are endemic, meaning they do not live anywhere else in the world. The area is home to a wide range of wildlife, including lemmings, brown bears, lynx, Siberian roe deer, wolves, and wild boar. Perhaps the most interesting mammal species found there is the nerpa, one of the world's only seals that lives entirely in freshwater.

Answer the items.

1. Do you think it is important for nations to work together to preserve places? Explain your answer.
   Answers will vary.

2. Why do you think some of Lake Baikal's plants and animals are endemic?
   Answers will vary.

Page 96

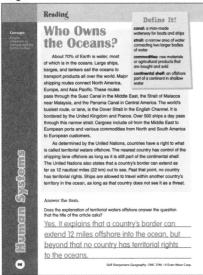

Reading

Who Owns the Oceans?

Define It!

canal: a man-made waterway for boats and ships

strait: a narrow area of water connecting two larger bodies of water

commodities: raw materials or agricultural products that are bought and sold

continental shelf: an offshore part of a continent in shallow water

About 70% of Earth is water, most of which is in the oceans. Large ships, barges, and tankers sail the oceans to transport products all over the world. Major shipping routes connect North America, Europe, and Asia Pacific. These routes pass through the Suez Canal in the Middle East, the Strait of Malacca near Malaysia, and the Panama Canal in Central America. The world's busiest route, or lane, is the Dover Strait in the English Channel. It is bordered by the United Kingdom and France. Over 500 ships a day pass through this narrow strait. Cargoes include oil from the Middle East to European ports and various commodities from North and South America to European customers.

As determined by the United Nations, countries have a right to what is called territorial waters offshore. The nearest country has control of the shipping lane offshore as long as it is still part of the continental shelf. The United Nations also states that a country's border can extend as far as 12 nautical miles (22 km) out to sea. Past that point, no country has territorial rights. Ships are allowed to travel within another country's territory in the ocean, as long as that country does not see it as a threat.

Answer the item.

Does the explanation of territorial waters offshore answer the question that the title of the article asks?

Yes, it explains that a country's border can extend 12 miles offshore into the ocean, but beyond that no country has territorial rights to the oceans.

Human Systems

96 Skill Sharpeners: Geography • EMC 3746 • © Evan-Moor Corp.

Page 98

Vocabulary Practice

By Land or By Sea?

Write the word next to its definition.

UNESCO tundra flora fauna endemic canal strait continental shelf

1. the animals of an area — fauna
2. a man-made waterway for ships — canal
3. a frozen grassland — tundra
4. a narrow area of water connecting larger bodies of water — strait
5. a group that helps preserve the world's special places — UNESCO
6. the plants of an area — flora
7. living only in that area — endemic
8. a part of a continent in shallow water — continental shelf

Think About It

Would you like to explore a special place in the world? Do you have an idea of where it may be? Why would you choose to go to that place?

Answers will vary.

Human Systems

98 Skill Sharpeners: Geography • EMC 3746 • © Evan-Moor Corp.

Page 100

Application

A Protected Place Near You

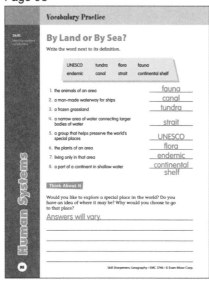

Is there a large area of land or water near you that is protected? What is special about it? If it isn't protected, should it be? Write to answer these questions and give your opinions.

Writing will vary.

Human Systems

100 Skill Sharpeners: Geography • EMC 3746 • © Evan-Moor Corp.

Page 102

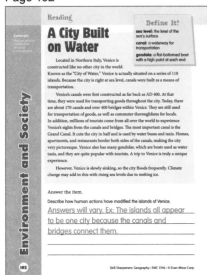

Reading

A City Built on Water

Define It!

sea level: the level of the sea's surface

canal: a waterway for transportation

gondola: a flat-bottomed boat with a high point at each end

Located in Northern Italy, Venice is constructed like no other city in the world. Known as the "City of Water," Venice is actually situated on a series of 118 islands. Because the city is right at sea level, canals were built as a means of transportation.

Venice's canals were first constructed as far back as AD 400. At that time, they were used for transporting goods throughout the city. Today, there are about 170 canals and over 400 bridges within Venice. They are still used for transportation of goods, as well as commuter thoroughfares for locals. In addition, millions of tourists come from all over the world to experience Venice's sights from the canals and bridges. The most important canal is the Grand Canal. It cuts the city in half and is used by water buses and taxis. Homes, apartments, and restaurants border both sides of the canals, making the city very picturesque. Venice also has many gondolas, which are boats used as water taxis, and they are quite popular with tourists. A trip to Venice is truly a unique experience.

However, Venice is slowly sinking, so the city floods frequently. Climate change may add to this with rising sea levels due to melting ice.

Answer the item.

Describe how human actions have modified the islands of Venice.

Answers will vary. Ex: The islands all appear to be one city because the canals and bridges connect them.

Environment and Society

102 Skill Sharpeners: Geography • EMC 3746 • © Evan-Moor Corp.

Page 104

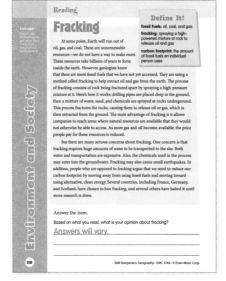

Reading

More Water Needed!

Define It!

reservoir: a man-made storage area for water

drought: a long period of dry weather

precipitation: rain, snow, sleet, or hail

The world's population is currently over 7.6 billion. With so many people on Earth, there is a need for more water. One way to get more water is to seed clouds.

Cloud seeding increases the amount of rain that storms produce. It is done primarily in areas where there are droughts. It is also done in locations where extra rain can be stored in reservoirs for times when there is little or no rainfall. China, the United States, and Australia are three countries known to use cloud seeding regularly, but it is also used elsewhere.

When there are storm clouds, a chemical called silver iodide is released into the clouds by planes or from the ground. The particles are similar to ice crystals. This makes water droplets in the clouds cling to the particles and become heavier, causing them to fall out of the clouds as rain or snow, or precipitation.

Cloud seeding can increase rainfall by about 10 to 20%. This means a place that gets around 20 inches (51 cm) of rain per year can increase its rainfall to 22 to 24 inches (56 to 61 cm). Over large areas and long periods of time, cloud seeding can help places that are dry get enough water.

Answer the item.

Do you think cloud seeding should be done more often or less often? Explain your answer.

Answers will vary.

Environment and Society

104 Skill Sharpeners: Geography • EMC 3746 • © Evan-Moor Corp.

Page 106

Vocabulary Practice

Dealing with Water

Solve this crossword puzzle using words related to water.

coral climate change sea level gondola cloud seed precipitation canal reservoir drought

Across

1. long period of dry weather
3. warmer temperatures now on Earth
6. rain, snow, sleet, or hail
7. hard material made from skeletons of marine organisms
8. man-made lake for storing water
9. waterway used for transportation

Down

2. special boat used as a taxi
4. to add chemicals to clouds to cause them to produce more precipitation
5. level of the ocean

Across: 1. drought 3. climatechange 6. precipitation 7. coral 8. reservoir 9. canal

Down: 2. gondola 4. cloudseed 5. sealevel

Environment and Society

106 Skill Sharpeners: Geography • EMC 3746 • © Evan-Moor Corp.

Page 108

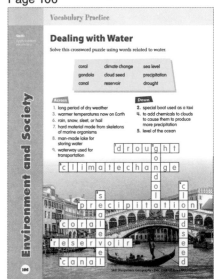

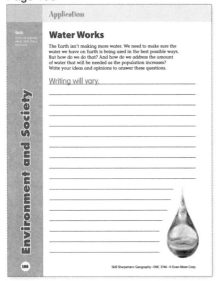

Application

Water Works

The Earth isn't making more water. We need to make sure the water we have on Earth is being used in the best possible ways. But how do we do that? And how do we address the amount of water that will be needed as the population increases? Write your ideas and opinions to answer these questions.

Writing will vary.

Environment and Society

108 Skill Sharpeners: Geography • EMC 3746 • © Evan-Moor Corp.

Page 110

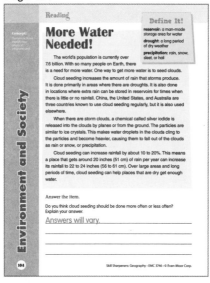

Reading

Fracking

Define It!

fossil fuels: oil, coal, and gas

fracking: spraying a high-powered mixture at rock to release oil and gas

carbon footprint: the amount of fossil fuels an individual person uses

At some point, Earth will run out of oil, gas, and coal. These are nonrenewable resources—we do not have a way to make more. These resources take billions of years to form inside the earth. However, geologists know that there are more fossil fuels that we have not yet accessed. They are using a method called fracking to help extract oil and gas from the earth. The process of fracking consists of rock being fractured apart by spraying a high-pressure mixture at it. Here's how it works: drilling pipes are placed deep in the ground, then a mixture of water, sand, and chemicals are sprayed at rocks underground. This process fractures the rocks, causing them to release oil or gas, which is then extracted from the ground. The main advantage of fracking is it allows companies to reach areas where natural resources are available that they would not otherwise be able to access. As more gas and oil become available, the price people pay for these resources is reduced.

But there are many serious concerns about fracking. One concern is that fracking requires huge amounts of water to be transported to the site. Both water and transportation are expensive. Also, the chemicals used in the process may enter into the groundwater. Fracking may also cause small earthquakes. In addition, people who are opposed to fracking argue that we need to reduce our carbon footprint by moving away from using fossil fuels and moving toward using alternative, clean energy. Several countries, including France, Germany, and Scotland, have chosen to ban fracking, and several others have halted it until more research is done.

Answer the item.

Based on what you read, what is your opinion about fracking?

Answers will vary.

Environment and Society

110 Skill Sharpeners: Geography • EMC 3746 • © Evan-Moor Corp.

Page 112

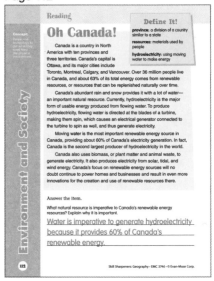

Reading

Oh Canada!

Define It!

province: a division of a country similar to a state

resources: materials used by people

hydroelectricity: using moving water to make energy

Canada is a country in North America with ten provinces and three territories. Canada's capital is Ottawa, and its major cities include Toronto, Montreal, Calgary, and Vancouver. Over 36 million people live in Canada, and about 63% of its total energy comes from renewable resources, or resources that can be replenished naturally over time.

Canada's abundant rain and snow provides it with a lot of water—an important natural resource. Currently, hydroelectricity is the major form of usable energy produced from flowing water. To produce hydroelectricity, flowing water is directed at the blades of a turbine, making them spin, which causes an electrical generator connected to the turbine to spin as well, and thus generate electricity.

Moving water is the most important renewable energy source in Canada, providing about 60% of Canada's electricity generation. In fact, Canada is the second largest producer of hydroelectricity in the world.

Canada also uses biomass, or plant matter and animal waste, to generate electricity. It also produces electricity from solar, tidal, and wind energy. Canada's focus on renewable energy sources will no doubt continue to power homes and businesses and result in even more innovations for the creation and use of renewable resources there.

Answer the item.

What natural resource is imperative to Canada's renewable energy resources? Explain why it is important.

Water is imperative to generate hydroelectricity because it provides 60% of Canada's renewable energy.

Environment and Society

112 Skill Sharpeners: Geography • EMC 3746 • © Evan-Moor Corp.

Page 114

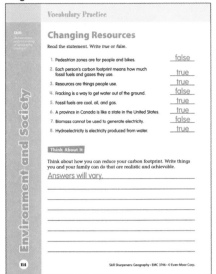

Changing Resources

Read the statement. Write *true* or *false*.

1. Pedestrian zones are for people and bikes. — false
2. Each person's carbon footprint means how much fossil fuels and gases they use. — true
3. Resources are things people use. — true
4. Fracking is a way to get water out of the ground. — false
5. Fossil fuels are coal, oil, and gas. — true
6. A province in Canada is like a state in the United States. — true
7. Biomass cannot be used to generate electricity. — false
8. Hydroelectricity is electricity produced from water. — true

Think About It

Think about how you can reduce your carbon footprint. Write things you and your family can do that are realistic and achievable.

Answers will vary.

Environment and Society

Page 116

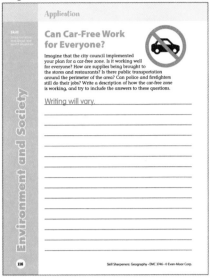

Can Car-Free Work for Everyone?

Imagine that the city council implemented your plan for a car-free zone. Is it working well for everyone? How are supplies being brought to the stores and restaurants? Is there public transportation around the perimeter of the area? Can police and firefighters still do their jobs? Write a description of how the car-free zone is working, and try to include the answers to these questions.

Writing will vary.

Environment and Society

Page 118

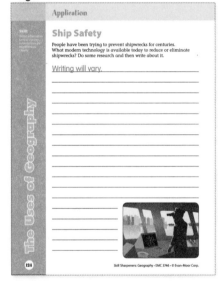

Sea Pirates

Define It!
Viking: a Scandinavian sea pirate and trader
merchant ship: a ship carrying valuables
bow and stern: the front and back of the boat

Long before the warship *Vasa* was built, Sweden, as well as the Scandinavian countries of Norway and Denmark, were known for Vikings. Vikings were sea pirates and traders, and they were also called seafaring warriors. They invaded coastal lands searching for treasures.

The Viking era began around the 8th century. It was around then that the Vikings' first raid surprised monks, who were chosen as victims because of their valuables and lack of defense. Many raids followed, occurring in Britain, northwest France, Ireland, and Scotland. Vikings also preyed upon merchant ships, which carried goods for trade. Vikings eventually settled in what is known today as parts of Russia, Iceland, Greenland, and Newfoundland, which is an island off the east coast of Canada.

Viking ships were designed to sail rough seas for long distances and to easily maneuver through difficult-to-navigate waters. The ships often had a trademark carved dragon's head or another circular object protruding from the bow and stern.

The Viking era continued until around the 11th century.

Answer the items.

1. Why do you think the Vikings lived as they did?
Answers will vary.

2. Why do you think Vikings used a trademark design on the front of their ships?
Answers will vary.

The Uses of Geography

Page 120

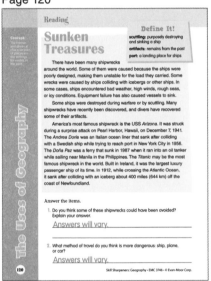

Sunken Treasures

Define It!
scuttling: purposely destroying and sinking a ship
artifacts: remains from the past
port: a landing place for ships

There have been many shipwrecks around the world. Some of them were caused because the ships were poorly designed, making them unstable for the load they carried. Some wrecks were caused by ships colliding with icebergs or other ships. In some cases, ships encountered bad weather, high winds, rough seas, or icy conditions. Equipment failure has also caused vessels to sink.

Some ships were destroyed during warfare or by scuttling. Many shipwrecks have recently been discovered, and divers have recovered some of their artifacts.

America's most famous shipwreck is the USS *Arizona*. It was struck during a surprise attack on Pearl Harbor, Hawaii, on December 7, 1941. The *Andrea Doria* was an Italian ocean liner that sank after colliding with a Swedish ship while trying to reach port in New York City in 1956. The *Doña Paz* was a ferry that sunk in 1987 when it ran into an oil tanker while sailing near Manila in the Philippines. The *Titanic* may be the most famous shipwreck in the world. Built in Ireland, it was the largest luxury passenger ship of its time. In 1912, while crossing the Atlantic Ocean, it sank after colliding with an iceberg about 400 miles (644 km) off the coast of Newfoundland.

Answer the items.

1. Do you think some of these shipwrecks could have been avoided? Explain your answer.
Answers will vary.

2. What method of travel do you think is more dangerous: ship, plane, or car?
Answers will vary.

The Uses of Geography

Page 122

Sea Travel

Read the statement. Write *true* or *false*.

1. Vikings are also known as sea pirates. — true
2. The bow and stern are the sides of a boat. — false
3. Merchant ships carry valuable items. — true
4. Scuttling is when ships sink due to bad weather. — false
5. Artifacts are natural items from the ocean. — false
6. A port is a landing place for ships. — true
7. Viking ships were not well-built. — false
8. Weather cannot cause a ship to sink. — false

Think About It

Since ships have sunk throughout history, what items do you think should be onboard all ships to make travel safer for the passengers and crew?

Answers will vary.

The Uses of Geography

Page 124

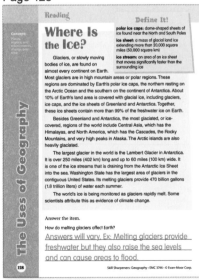

Ship Safety

People have been trying to prevent shipwrecks for centuries. What modern technology is available today to reduce or eliminate shipwrecks? Do some research and then write about it.

Writing will vary.

The Uses of Geography

Page 126

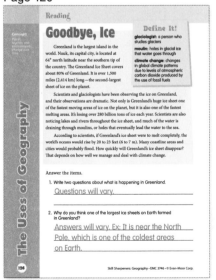

Goodbye, Ice

Define It!
glaciologist: a person who studies glaciers
moulin: holes in glacial ice that water goes through
climate change: changes in global climate patterns due to levels of atmospheric carbon dioxide produced by the use of fossil fuels

Greenland is the largest island in the world. Nuuk, its capital city, is located at 64° north latitude near the southern tip of the country. The Greenland Ice Sheet covers about 80% of Greenland. It is over 1,500 miles (2,414 km) long—the second-largest sheet of ice on the planet.

Scientists and glaciologists have been observing the ice on Greenland, and their observations are dramatic. Not only is Greenland's huge ice sheet one of the fastest moving areas of ice on the planet, but it is also one of the fastest melting areas. It's losing over 280 billion tons of ice each year. Scientists are also noticing lakes and rivers throughout the ice sheet, and much of the water is draining through moulins, or holes that eventually lead the water to the sea.

According to scientists, if Greenland's ice sheet were to melt completely, the world's oceans would rise by 20 to 23 feet (6 to 7 m). Many coastline areas and cities would probably flood. How quickly will Greenland's ice sheet disappear? That depends on how well we manage and deal with climate change.

Answer the items.

1. Write two questions about what is happening in Greenland.
Questions will vary.

2. Why do you think one of the largest ice sheets on Earth formed in Greenland?
Answers will vary. Ex: It is near the North Pole, which is one of the coldest areas on Earth.

The Uses of Geography

Page 128

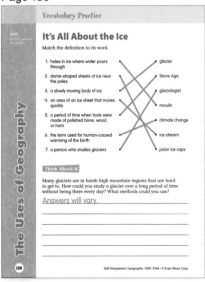

Where Is the Ice?

Define It!
polar ice caps: dome-shaped sheets of ice found near the North and South Poles
ice sheet: a mass of glacial land ice extending more than 20,000 square miles (50,000 square km)
ice stream: an area of an ice sheet that moves significantly faster than the surrounding ice

Glaciers, or slowly moving bodies of ice, are found on almost every continent on Earth. Most glaciers are in high mountain areas or polar regions. These regions are dominated by Earth's polar ice caps, the northern resting on the Arctic Ocean and the southern on the continent of Antarctica. About 10% of Earth's land area is covered with glacial ice, including glaciers, ice caps, and the ice sheets of Greenland and Antarctica. Together, these ice sheets contain more than 99% of the freshwater ice on Earth.

Besides Greenland and Antarctica, the most glaciated, or ice-covered, regions of the world include Central Asia, which has the Himalayas, and North America, which has the Cascades, the Rocky Mountains, and very high peaks in Alaska. The Arctic islands are also heavily glaciated.

The largest glacier in the world is the Lambert Glacier in Antarctica. It is over 250 miles (402 km) long and up to 60 miles (100 km) wide. It is one of the ice streams that is draining from the Antarctic Ice Sheet into the sea. Washington State has the largest area of glaciers in the contiguous United States. Its melting glaciers provide 470 billion gallons (1.8 trillion liters) of water each summer.

The world's ice is being monitored as glaciers rapidly melt. Some scientists attribute this as evidence of climate change.

Answer the item.

How do melting glaciers affect Earth?
Answers will vary. Ex: Melting glaciers provide freshwater but they also raise the sea levels and can cause areas to flood.

The Uses of Geography

Page 130

It's All About the Ice

Match the definition to its word.

1. holes in ice where water pours through — glacier
2. dome-shaped sheets of ice near the poles — Stone Age
3. a slowly moving body of ice — glaciologist
4. an area of an ice sheet that moves quickly — moulin
5. a period of time when tools were made of polished bone, wood, or horn — climate change
6. the term used for human-caused warming of the Earth — ice stream
7. a person who studies glaciers — polar ice caps

Think About It

Many glaciers are in harsh high mountain regions that are hard to get to. How could you study a glacier over a long period of time without being there every day? What methods could you use?

Answers will vary.

The Uses of Geography

Page 132

Application

Skill
Write to share
observations

Signs of Warmth

Many scientists who are studying climate change agree that Earth is getting warmer due in part to human activity. Many point to melting glaciers as evidence. But what other evidence could there be? Can you think of other data or observations that might indicate a warmer Earth? Write about the other evidence and your observations.

The Uses of Geography

Skill Sharpeners: Geography • EMC 3746 • © Evan-Moor Corp.

Notes

Notes

Notes